Greek
Mythology

LIBRARY OF THE WORLD'S
MYTHS AND LEGENDS

Greek Mythology

John Pinsent

NEWNES BOOKS

Half title page. Reverse of four drachma piece of Acragas, 420–415 B.C. The symbols of the city of Acragas were the eagle of Zeus, in whose honour the people built a colossal temple, and the crab, which, perhaps because it was proverbial for crooked dealing, they later supplemented with a fish or other symbol of the sea. On this coin they added the sea monster Scylla, who lived in the straits of Messina. Her name means 'whelp', and there is no trace here of the six heads on long necks which devoured six of Odysseus' men. As always, the monsters of Greek art are more human than those of literature. Private collection.

Frontispiece. White-figure vase showing the infant Dionysus and Father Silenus. Musei Vaticani.

Greek Mythology first published 1969.
New revised edition
published 1982 by Newnes Books,
a division of The Hamlyn Publishing Group Limited,
84–88 The Centre, Feltham, Middlesex, TW13 4BH,
and distributed for them by
The Hamlyn Publishing Group Limited,
Rushden, Northants, England

ISBN 0 600 34278 6

Printed in Yugoslavia

Contents

Introduction

There is a great deal of Greek mythology, and this book does not contain it all. Almost all Greek art and literature either took its subjects from mythology or made reference to it. The Greeks told stories about the family life of the gods, and they had a myth about the creation of the world and how the present dynasty of the gods came to power; but most of their mythology is concerned with the heroic world. This world joined on to the historical world of the Greeks in time. It came to an end with the return of the children of Heracles to the Peloponnese, the mythological equivalent of the Dorian invasion, when the last wave of Greek-speaking peoples entered Greece and settled in Boeotia and Sparta. The Spartan kings traced their descent back to these children of Heracles.

For the Greeks, heroic mythology was ancient history. They constructed genealogies which related all the human personages of the myths, and prepared schematic mythological handbooks to explain references in the older authors. In the earlier periods, writers felt free to improve and even invent myths, doubtless maintaining that they were simply telling for the first time the real truth. Their inventions, however, tended to follow the patterns of existing myths.

Such patterns are the first thing that strikes the student of Greek mythology. The second is the extraordinary character of its content. It is all about homicides, exiles, quarrels, seductions and illegitimate births, many of them taking place inside the family circle. Greek mythology has its share of monsters, but the humanist outlook of the Greeks generally rejected magic. In other respects the myths do resemble fairy tales.

Above. The young Apollo. The central figure of the western pediment of the fifth-century temple of Zeus at Olympia was Apollo, subduing a Centaur. Archaeological Museum, Olympia.

Left. Mount Olympus in Thessaly, the seat of the gods.

Opposite. Bronze Core. This 6-inch (15 cm) statuette of about 480 B.C. was very possibly identified as a goddess by some emblem, now lost, in the right hand. It is more probable perhaps that it represented the donor perpetually offering whatever it was she held. Traces of silver inlay remain on the fringe of her dress as she holds it aside. At this stage in the development of the art drapery is beautifully handled to suggest clearly the human form beneath, a technique which was more easily handled in bronze than in stone. British Museum, London.

A label is not, however, an explanation. One of the commonest of such motifs is the tale of the young man who goes on a journey to a far country where he is set a number of tasks or quests in order to win the hand of a maiden who is the daughter either of a king or of an enchanter. Success brings him the kingdom sometimes at the cost of the death of the enchanter, and he lives happily ever after.

This pattern recurs in Greek mythology with some significant differences. The young man usually leaves home because of a family quarrel or homicide, sometimes provoked by a step-mother. The father of the princess is often afraid of death at the hands of his daughter's husband, and himself engages in a contest with her suitors. In other cases it is his daughter's son that represents the threat, and the child, almost always the son of a god, is exposed (occasionally with his mother) to be miraculously preserved and often suckled by wild beasts. In the end he brings about his grandfather's death after having acquired a bride in the usual way.

There is little doubt that all these stories are still told because they satisfy some psychological need in the minds of their hearers. Psychological explanations, usually Freudian, can be found for many myths and some have been proposed in this book. But the familiarity of the pattern sometimes obscures its chief characteristic: that sons never inherit from fathers. Many of the more unpleasant features of the myths fall into place if they are seen as descriptions of what inheritance in the female line looked like to people who practised patrilinear

succession themselves. This hypothesis finds some support in the number of Greek heroes who marry their brother's daughter.

The study of mythology seems to encourage the pursuit of extravagant speculations that go far beyond the evidence. It is for the poet and the novelist, not for the scholar, to see mother-goddesses everywhere. None the less it seems possible that some of the Greek myths do preserve traces of a period in which kings owed their title to marriage with a queen, and were liable to be violently overthrown at the end of a period either by a new consort or by their daughter's husband, who was, of course, completely unrelated to them by blood. Some myths suggest that the king impersonated a god who might also appear as an animal, and that in the end he was made immortal by sacrifice, a fate which he could sometimes avoid by the sacrifice of his son.

If this state of affairs ever prevailed in Greece it was during, and perhaps early during, the Mycenaean period and its immediate predecessors, after Greek-speaking people had entered Greece in about 2100 or 1900 B.C., when there seems to have been a cultural break which did not affect Crete in the same way. It was not congenial to the writers of Greek literature – the archaic and classical Greeks of the period from about 1000 B.C. when Mycenaean civilisation, which had extended to Crete about 1400 B.C. or a century or so later, disappeared. Until recently the decline of Mycenaean civilisation was seen as destruction by invading Dorians, who spoke a different form of Greek and to whom were attributed certain cultural innovations – iron and cremation. Some scholars would still accept some elements of this view. But the Dorians have never been archaeologically visible (one recent view sees them as the Mycenaean Proletariat), and it may be better to think in terms of a change in social organisation consequent on the break-up of Mycenaean palace economy for economic and political reasons. These may account for a new form of social organisation, based upon the small nuclear family, in which an autocratic father rules over his wife and the children of the marriage.

The tensions that arise in this type of family are reflected in some of the myths and in the literature of classical Greece, especially in Greek tragedy. Such a culture may be called a 'guilt culture', where moral sanctions are enforced by an internalised super-ego based on the child's experience of its father. It superseded a 'shame culture' characteristic of the extended family, in which the child is brought up in an atmosphere of diffused benevolence by its brothers, sisters and cousins, and so learns to rely entirely upon the approval and disapproval of its peers. In such a culture men project their rapidly changing emotions upon a world of gods, and feel neither responsibility nor guilt themselves. This type of culture is reflected in the Homeric epics, and the Greeks always retained elements of it. It too is reflected in some of the myths.

It is explanations of this kind, psychological, anthropological and sociological, which are tentatively suggested, along with others more traditional, in this book, because they seem best to account for some of the peculiarities of the Greek myths.

The Ancient Sources

1. The *Iliad* and the *Odyssey*, the oldest surviving works of Greek literature, are both popularly attributed to one man, Homer, but the *Odyssey* is probably a good deal later than the *Iliad*. Both are organisations of older traditional material, first carried out in Asia Minor from about 800 B.C. but perhaps not reaching its present final form until the Athens of Pisistratus in the six century.

2. Hesiod is the author of the *Works and Days*, a didactic poem addressed to his brother, with whom he had quarrelled over their inheritance. His father had returned from Asia Minor to Boeotia, where there seems to have been a school of epic poetry especially devoted to lists and catalogues. The mythological poem, the *Theogony*, is generally attributed to Hesiod, but seems rather to be the work of one of his successors, who starts the poem with an account of his graduation in the poetical school of Hesiod, perhaps as early as the eighth century.

3. Pindar's *Victory Odes*, addressed to winners in the Olympic and other Greek games, are the largest body of lyric poetry with mythological content. He made use, in the first half of the fifth century, of the mythological traditions known to the Homeric poets and gathered together by their epic successors and earlier lyric poets. He sometimes expurgated or invented myths to accord with his lofty ethical principles. His younger contemporary Bacchylides wrote similar odes telling the myths in a more straightforward manner.

4. The great Athenian tragedians of the fifth century, Aeschylus, Sophocles and Euripides, took their plots from the same sources as Pindar and used them to express their views of the nature of the world and its gods. Sometimes they used aetiological myths, which explain a particular ritual by an account of its institution. They too modified and invented myths to suit their own purposes.

5. The systematisation of mythology, often on genealogical or local principles, began as early as the sixth century in Asia Minor. It was carried a stage further by the scholars and poets of Alexandria, the city founded in Egypt by Alexander the Great after his conquest of that country and the rest of the Persian Empire. Ruling minorities among an alien culture find it necessary to assert that of their own origins, especially when that culture is no longer as creative as was that of archaic Greece and fifth-century Athens, and the way this was done in Alexandria was by learned commentary and imitation of earlier poetry. The surviving works of Apollonius Rhodius and Callimachus exemplify this use of myth, which has more in common with that of Roman poets and of European poets of the Renaissance and later than it does with the earlier period of Greek literature. But they do preserve much mythological information otherwise unknown.

6. Pausanias wrote a literary and artistic guidebook to Greece in about A.D. 170. He told the mythical history of all the places he visited, drawing his material from Athenian and Alexandrian genealogical studies. He also reports all local ceremonies and myths, which are extremely valuable, since they represent the beliefs and practice of the ordinary Greeks, less affected by literary treatments of myth.

7. Apollodorus wrote a *Library* of mythological information, arranged genealogically, about the same date. It is the only complete surviving Greek account of mythology, and is therefore, though a summary, extremely useful. In some cases, however, its stories are based on tragic or invented Alexandrian versions of the myth, and it should therefore be treated with caution.

It would be invidious to single out any of the many modern translations of these works. The Victorian translations of the *Iliad* by Lang, Leaf and Myers and of the *Odyssey* by Butcher and Lang preserve the flavour of the original.

And the annotated translation of Apollodorus made for the Loeb Library by Sir James G. Frazer deserves special mention. Frazer's theories, to be found in the *Golden Bough,* are nowadays unfashionable; but his translation still contains a lot of good sense on mythology.

There is no good modern mythological dictionary in English. The old three volume *Dictionary of Greek and Roman Biography and Mythology,* edited by William Smith in 1876, is still more exhaustive than the late H. J. Rose's useful *Handbook of Greek Mythology.*

The Origins of the World

When primitive peoples ask questions about the creation of the world they normally answer them in one of two ways. Either the gods made the world as a carpenter makes a chair out of wood, or they begot it as a father begets his children. These are primitive answers with strong psychological overtones, because the disquiet, which these answers are given to settle, itself stems from a primitive level of the mind, and is therefore best satisfied by an answer given in those terms. It is at this level that much myth and literature is effective.

The Creation Myth

In Hesiod's cosmogony, first there were Chaos and Earth. From Chaos came Erebus and Night; from Night the Ether (upper air) and Day. Earth first produced the Sea, then Ocean, and then the Titans, Coeus, Crius, Hyperion, Iapetus, Theia, Rhea, Themis, Mnemosyne, Phoebe, Tethys, and finally Cronus. Many of these figures are nothing more than personifications: Themis is a divine Ordinance; Mnemosyne is Memory, mother of the Muses; Hyperion, 'he that goes over', is the sun; and Phoebe, 'shining', is the moon. Oceanus is distinguished from Pontus, the sea. He is the stream which girdles the circular earth and beyond which man cannot sail because there is nothing there except Hades. Those who live on the streams of Ocean, from which the sun rises and into which he sets, returning every night in a golden bowl, presumably on Ocean, are superior beings, and are visited by the immortals. Such are the blameless Ethiopians in the south and the virtuous Hyperboreans in the north, who live beyond the North Wind.

There are traces in Homer that Ocean once played a larger role in an alternative cosmology. There are two references in the *Iliad* to 'Ocean, the source of the gods, and mother Tethys,' and one to 'Ocean, who has been made the source of all things'. This 'wet' cosmology seems to be Egyptian and Babylonian, where earth appears from the receding flood waters of the (male) rivers which penetrate the (female) salt sea. In the drier lands of Greece the 'dry' cosmology prevailed, when the (female) earth is fertilised by the rain from a (male) heaven. It may have been Ocean, rather than Poseidon, the later god of the sea, who first bore the Homeric title 'earth-holder, shaker of earth': for Ocean surrounds the earth and keeps it in place, so that like the earth snake of Norse mythology he could easily also cause it to quake.

The Succession Myth

It is after this schematic creation myth that the *Theogony* becomes more naturalistic, and has psychological overtones derived perhaps from the 'primal scene' of parental intercourse as witnessed by the child, as well as from the infant fear of its huge and capricious parents armed, as it is not, with gnashing teeth. Children can be observed to take an ambiguous pleasure in biting games with their parents, who pretend to eat them up, and these reactions illuminate the

Opposite. Temple of Apollo, Corinth. This, the chief temple of the city, survived from about 540 B.C., when it was built at the height of Corinthian commercial power, to the Roman conquest of 146 B.C. when it was burnt out. But the columns survived, to make Corinth one of the most impressive sites of antiquity. Seven still remain at the south-west corner.

myth of Cronus and Uranus, 'Heaven', and Gaia, 'Earth'.

Uranus hated his children and as soon as each was born he hid him away in a hiding place of Earth and would not let him come into the light. The huge Earth groaned in pain and devised an evil trick. First she made adamant, and from it a sickle, and called upon her children to take vengeance on their lewd father for his evil treatment of them. Only the youngest, Cronus of the bent counsel, had the courage to respond, and promised to do the deed. Earth took him into her bed, with the sickle in his hand. When Uranus returned, bringing night, he lay upon Earth in desire, and she was stretched out beneath him. Cronus reached out with his left hand and seized his father, and with his right he castrated him with the sickle and flung the parts behind him with averted eyes. Blood gushed forth upon Earth, and from it in due course she bore the Furies and the Giants, and the Ash nymphs, from whom the gods made the third race of men, the Bronze men.

But the parts fell on the sea, and from the bloody foam was made a maiden, and first she sailed to Cythera and then to Cyprus. There the fair goddess stepped from the sea, and grass grew under her soft feet, and gods and men call her Aphrodite, that is, 'Foam born'. This is a piece of folk etymology for there is another and in some ways more plausible account of

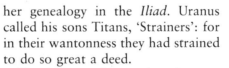

her genealogy in the *Iliad*. Uranus called his sons Titans, 'Strainers': for in their wantonness they had strained to do so great a deed.

The Ash nymphs are there because an ash plantation can, by suitable management and regular if not annual cutting down, be made to yield a supply of tough, straight, strong stems for spear hafts, like the ashy stem of Peleus which only his son Achilles could wield. A race of spear-using heroes might well be made from the same wood as their weapons, and the regular pruning may have contributed something to the myth of castration. But there seems to have been some expurgation. It is not so much that Uranus hides away a born child as that his continued intercourse with earth blocks the birth passage; 'castration' as for Freud, seems to mean also the removal of the penis, a fear often fantasised in intercourse.

There are parallels to this myth in the Near East in the second millennium. Texts survive from about 1200 B.C. from the Hittite capital in Asia Minor; these contain a Succession

Myth, as it is generally called, taken over from the Hurrians of south-eastern Asia Minor. This tells how Anu the sky god overthrew Alalu and reigned for nine years, after which Kumarbi strove with him, chased him to heaven, bit off his genitals and swallowed them, but spat out part from which a god Tamisu and the river Tigris were born.

A similar story, but earlier, is preserved in various fragments from the official text used at the Babylonian New Year Festival. In this the first divine pair are Apsu, god of the fresh water, and Tiamat, the sea goddess, who initiate a genealogy of gods who all remain inside the mingled waters of their parents. Anu the sky god is their great-grandson and Ea is his son. This family in some way disturbed Tiamat, and Apsu resolved to destroy them, against her will. They fell silent and Ea cast a magic spell upon Apsu, stripped him of his regalia and his strength, and slew him. In this version the separation of heaven and earth do not come until later: in the Hittite it is not mentioned and appears to be prior to the story.

The resemblance to the Greek myth, is certainly close, and extends also to the myth of the overthrow of Cronus by Zeus. Various theories have been put forward how and when direct or indirect borrowing might have taken place, either during the Mycenaean period of the Bronze Age before 1200 B.C. or in the eighth century 'orientalising period' of Greek art. There can be little doubt that versions of earlier and eastern stories were known to the tellers of versions of the Greek cosmogonies and have influenced them. Oceanus and Tethys in the alternative cosmogony of the *Iliad* mentioned above strongly suggest Apsu and Tiamat. Their estrangement suggests the separation of heaven and earth which is often felt as implicit in the mutilation of Uranus.

The castration of Anu by Kumarbi, and the generation of a god and of the Tigris in the Hittite myth similarly suggest the Greek, and may have been edited out of the Babylonian to appear innocuously as a magic sleep and the theft of the regalia. But Earth plays no part in either of these other versions, and it is to her presence that the Greek version owes the strong human and psychological overtones which give it a quality quite lacking in those of others.

The Oedipal element in the Greek myth is so strong as to suggest that it can have arisen only in the period of the guilt culture derived from the nuclear family. The elements may have been borrowed from the east, but the psychology of the stories is purely Greek. Much of the cosmological significance of the myth is obscured in what appears rather as a classical Oedipal fantasy, in which the child succeeds in supplanting the father in his mother's bed with her connivance. Hesiod does not say why father and son were so hostile: in fact they are rivals for the love of the mother.

Such is the explanation that can be given at one level of the myth: others are not excluded. For Uranus is cut with the sickle, an instrument which however well suited for the purpose may legitimately suggest that the story has been also influenced by stories of the annual sacrifice of the corn

or its representative. As always in Greek myth, with its complicated history, no one explanation may contain all the truth.

The Birth of Zeus

The overtones so strong in the first part of the Greek succession myth are absent from the second. This time the successful victor is Zeus, high god of the Greeks, and any suggestion of mutilation has been completely suppressed, or perhaps displaced to the previous generation, where it could safely be attributed to Uranus. There were indeed legends that the reign of Zeus was not entirely secure, and that he feared he might be supplanted in his turn. But he always succeeded in averting this fate.

The *Theogony* tells how Rhea bore Cronus a number of children – Hestia, Demeter, Hera and Hades, all of whom he swallowed, knowing that he would be supplanted by his son. When the youngest, Zeus, was going to be born, Rhea was sent by Gaia and Uranus to Crete where she had the child in a cave near Lyctus and gave Cronus a stone to swallow.

The poet brings in Uranus and Gaia to explain why Cronus in his turn hated his children. They advised Rhea how to outwit him in order that Zeus might do the bidding of the Furies that sprang from the blood of Uranus. Fate is thus invoked to remove the responsibility of parricide from Zeus. The birth of Zeus took place in Crete because the Cretans gave the name of Zeus to the young consort of one of their mother-goddesses, perhaps the Earth mother, and also acquired their proverbial fame as liars by pointing out the tomb of Zeus.

The name Zeus is firmly Greek, and so it must have been Greeks in Crete, and not Minoans, who made the identification. But the cave near Lyctus was superseded after the Bronze Age. This story must go back to that period when Greeks were in Crete in the Mycenaean age, though they were clearly ready to modify the position and fate of their chief god into the dying consort of the Cretan goddess. The infant Zeus was fed by the milk of Amalthea the goat and on the honey of bees, while his cradle was hung on a tree 'that it might be found neither in heaven nor in earth nor in the sea'. His cries were drowned by the armed dance of the Young Men, the Curetes, who clashed their arms in Cretan ritual.

Zeus grew rapidly and Earth helped him to overthrow Cronus. Cronus vomited up his children and last of all the stone, which Zeus set at Delphi. Again the help of the mother is enlisted to rescue the son, but the machinery is left perhaps deliberately obscure. On the analogy of the Babylonian myth, in which it is at this point that Marduk son of Ea splits the body of Tiamat to make heaven and earth, it might be supposed that Zeus slit open his father like a fairy tale hero. In the Hittite version the weather god who is the equivalent of Zeus is still inside Kumarbi, where he was engendered by the swallowed genitals of Anu. For some reason Kumarbi swallows a stone, after which the god emerges to engage in battle.

Once again the differences are as striking as the similarities. The Greek myth concentrates its attention upon the stone, which is identified as the sacred stone of Delphi. According to other versions this was the navel stone of earth (metaphorically rather than literally) which marked its dead centre. Zeus sent two eagles flying, one from the east and one from the west: they met over Delphi. It is natural for men to think of their own land as the centre of the earth, and Delphi was becoming an important cult centre at the time of the *Theogony*.

The Titans

One final parallel exists between the Greek cosmological myths and those of the Near East. This is the need for the newly triumphant god to defend his position first against gods and then against monsters sent up against him by Earth. The former are found only in the Greek and Hittite myths: in the Greek the gods are the Titans, who presumably resented the overthrow of their brother Cronus. But the battle, which lasted ten years, may have started as a revolt of the younger gods. They expelled the Titans from Olympus, for the possession of which the battle was fought in the plains of Thessaly.

At this stage Earth was still on the side of Zeus and advised him that he could defeat the Titans with the help of the three Cyclops and the three Hundred-handers, her children by Uranus who had never been released. So, it seems, was Oceanus, to whom Rhea entrusted Hera at this time, according to the alternative 'cosmogony'. This is explicable if in this version Oceanus played the part of Uranus.

It is a common motif in myth that a great enterprise cannot be completed without the presence of a Helper, often specially endowed with particular talents or weapons. The Hundred-handers played this role in the battle of the Titans, and it was their ability between them to hurl three hundred rocks at a time which enabled them to rout and pursue the Titans to Tartarus. There they guarded them for Zeus, though there is a nasty suspicion that the Hundred-handers were prisoners as well as warders.

Since the world is to be regarded as a sphere, divided into two equal hemispheres by a flat circular earth surrounded by Ocean, Tartarus, which seems to be the bottom of the underworld, approaches earth at the west. For the underworld is often reached from the west, the region of the setting sun, rather than from any other of the theoretically possible points of the compass. Atlas stood in the west in the sea that is beyond Ocean, and is called Atlantic after him. He bore on his shoulders either the heaven or the two pillars which kept apart earth and heaven. There

too the Hesperides guarded the golden apples. At a later stage Atlas was identified with the mountain that still bears his name in North Africa, just as his pillars were taken over by Heracles at the Straits of Gibraltar. Atlas was said to have been turned into stone by the Gorgon's head, but not by Perseus since Heracles, Perseus' great grandson, sent him for the golden apples.

As early as the *Odyssey* the underworld has four great rivers, all suitably named. Most important is Styx, 'Hateful', which was identified with an icy waterfall in Arcadia, presumably one of the underworld entrances. By Styx the gods swore their most binding oath, to break which entailed keeping silence for a year and exile for nine (eight years by our reckoning: this is a great year, when all the stars and planets return to their original position, a period that recurs in Greek myth and ritual). Probably Styx was once the only river of Hades, since Cocytus, 'Wailing for the dead', is said to be its tributary. The other two rivers are Acheron (*Achos* means pain; but the white poplar, *acherois*, like the white willow, seems to have been sacred to Persephone) and Pyriphlegethon, 'burning with the pyre'. The fifth river Lethe, first in Aristophanes, seems to be associated with reincarnation and a spring of memory.

Typhon

Earth was shocked by the punishment of her sons the Titans, and, as she had done once before, shifted her allegiance. She bore a youngest son Typhoeus, or Typhon, a serpent man who might be expected to continue the succession. Against Typhon Zeus employed for the first time the thunder and lightning that the Cyclops had made him, and pinned him under the volcano Etna. But the victory may not have been as easy as the *Theogony* suggests. The version of Apollodorus says that Typhon was born in Cilicia, where he fathered monsters on the Gorgon's sister, the snake woman Echidna: their children were Orthus, the monstrous hound of three-bodied Geryon, Cerberus, the

Hydra and the Chimaera. Zeus pursued him to the borders of Syria with an adamantine sickle, probably the one with which Cronus mutilated Uranus, where he grappled with him. Typhon got the sickle and cut out the sinews from Zeus' hands and feet, disabling him and putting him in a cave in Cilicia where he hid the sinews in a bearskin watched over by a serpent woman Delphyna. But Hermes stole them and revived Zeus, who flew to heaven in a winged chariot and pursued Typhon again to Mount Nysa (which recurs in the legend of Dionysus) where the fates weakened him by giving him mortal food. It was only then that Zeus could drive him to Etna by way of Thrace where his blood marked the Bloody Mountain, Haemus.

Opposite. Zeus brandishing a thunderbolt. This 6-inch (15 cm) statuette from Dodona almost exactly reproduces the pose of the 'Poseidon' of very much the same date, about 460 B.C. The single difference is that the short heavy thunderbolt (which identifies Zeus) is thrown with a bent arm, unlike the longer javelin. Dodona was the site of a very ancient oracular shrine of Zeus the thunder god, who gave omens by the rustling of the leaves of the sacred oak tree. Thunderstorms are extremely common on the mountains of north-western Greece, and the oak tree is more frequently struck by the lightning than any other tree. Antikenmuseum, Berlin.

Below. Zeus and Typhon. In the last half of the sixth century a distinctive school of vase painting developed, probably in Etruria, though the artists were Greeks from Euboean colonies in Sicily. Their mythological illustrations are strong and vivid. Zeus is attacking the giant Typhon with a thunderbolt. Typhon is shown as a huge figure with a bestial face and pointed ears, wings and a double serpent below the waist. The poets were able to make his description even more fantastic, attributing to him a hundred serpent heads under his shoulders. Zeus' left leg is restored. Staatliche Antikensammlungen und Glyptothek, Munich.

The Greeks certainly explained vol-
canoes as the work of fire-breathing
monsters imprisoned under the earth.
The theft of Zeus' sinews is paralleled
in the Hittite myth of the encounter
with the dragon Illuyankas, who
takes the god's heart and eyes. His
son gets them back by marrying the
dragon's daughter. This fairy tale motif is absent from the Greek version,
where the task is performed by the
Thief God. Also in the Hittite, the
giant Ullikummi is only countered by
sawing off his legs with the bronze
cutter that severed earth and heaven

in the beginning. All this suggests a
version of the succession myth with
the persons and the results altered to
make it applicable to the surviving
god, who wins the contest and even
survives castration.

Temple of Aphaea, Aegina. The goddess
Aphaea seems to have been a form of the
pre-Greek mother-goddess, and in myth
she was associated with Artemis. Her
temple lay on the main mountain range
of the island, at its north-east end, and
gives views of the island of Salamis to
the north. The classical town of Aegina
lay on the west of the island, looking to
Epidaurus, and the isolation of the
temple, appropriate to a nature goddess,
has preserved the building. The temple
was built about 510 B.C., just before the
struggle of the Aeginetans with the
expanding Athenians. The goddess
seems later to have been identified in cult
with Athena, either to symbolise the link
between the two cities or at the desire of
a pro-Athenian party.

The Family of the Gods

In this way Zeus broke the succession cycle and established his role. There are, however, persistent hints in the myths both that Zeus feared in his turn being overthrown by his son and also that some of the gods tried to cast him down. The world was then divided between the three sons of Cronus, Zeus, Poseidon and Hades. In the *Theogony*, it is Zeus who assigns the blessed gods their honours. In the *Iliad* Poseidon describes the division of the patrimony among the three sons of a father who has retired from active life, though he is not necessarily dead. There is no trace either of primogeniture (succession of the eldest son) or of ultimogeniture (succession of the youngest son).

A number of these terracotta reliefs from Locri in South Italy are shown in this book, for their combination of high artistic quality and strong religious feeling. The cult to which they relate has not yet been fully explained, and their subjects are not always clear. Here a woman offers a cock and an object that might (and should) be a pomegranate, to a seated goddess, to whom there has already been presented a folded robe, which rests on a table under which is a bird which looks more like a duck, goose or swan than an eagle. That could identify the goddess as Aphrodite: other suggestions are Koré (or even her mother Demeter), or Hera, a popular goddess in Italy. But the problem is only one of name: the cults were much concerned with love and death, both actual and the death to the old self implied in marriage.

Left. The Sacred Marriage of Zeus and Hera. The German excavations in the sanctuary of Hera on Samos, which started in the 1930s, revealed some of the few surviving Greek wooden statues, though it has not always been possible to save them from disintegration. The late sixth-century bridal pair, now lost, probably represents the Sacred Marriage, but in a style which suggests the love of the divine couple when they were still young and in the house of their parents, before Zeus overthrew Cronus and claimed the sovereignty. Attention is focused on the breasts of the goddess, as in the terracotta protome of Persephone or Demeter on page 24.

Above. The Twelve Olympians. As the expanding Greek cities absorbed their smaller neighbours together with the local cults, they set up an official state cult of the Twelve Olympians to express this new sense of unity. An early fifth-century relief, said to come from Tarentum, shows that the cult also spread to the rich Greek colonies in Sicily and southern Italy founded at the end of the eighth century. Apollo with his lyre leads the procession with Artemis and her bow. Then comes Zeus with the thunderbolt, Athena with her owl, Poseidon with the trident, Hera, Hades and Persephone, who carries the ears of corn, helmetted Ares with Aphrodite holding a flower, Hermes in cap and with his wand, the caduceus, and finally a figure with a basket who is probably Demeter.

Opposite. Zeus and Hera. The Greek city of Selinus in the extreme south-west of Sicily owed its prosperity to its links with Carthage. From the end of the sixth century it built an impressive series of temples which have been preserved by their isolation. The mid-fifth century temple E seems to have been dedicated to Hera. The metopes were placed not in the open on the façade but on the ends of the interior building, the *cella*. They show encounters between male and female gods and heroes: the female heads, arms and feet are of marble carved by a different and superior sculptor. On this metope the goddess Hera unveils herself for Zeus as a bride: the Sacred Marriage has been humanised. Museo Nazionale, Palermo.

There are indeed traces in Greek mythology of what may be called the Indo-European family of the gods: that is, of a family of gods organised upon patriarchal principles. But among Greeks it is complicated by assimilation to religious systems indigenous to Greece.

Zeus and Hera

The word *Zeus* is connected with the first part of the Latin Jupiter and with the word for *day*. He is the sky god of the bright sky, but also of the storm, and so is armed with the thunderbolt. He might be expected to have an exactly equivalent consort, and so he has in one myth: Dione, the mother of Aphrodite. Dione's name is the exact counterpart of his own and is related to the Latin Juno (who is also the Etruscan Uni).

But generally in mythology Zeus' consort is Hera. Her name seems to be the feminine of 'hero' and to mean 'the lady'. This is a perfectly proper title for the wife of the chief god. But Hera had a cult of her own in Argos and is unquestionably a survival of one of the indigenous mother-goddesses of Greece. As such, she is closely associated with young heroes such as, originally, Heracles, who is named after her 'glory of Hera', and also Jason. Otherwise, she appears almost exclusively as the jealous wife resentful of her husband's amours and bastards (of whom, in the developed legend, Heracles was one). Indeed, in an amusing passage of the *Iliad*, Zeus invites Hera to bed, saying that he loves her more than any of a list of seven women, two of them goddesses. This is in fact part of a Boeotian catalogue of what the *Odyssey* calls 'wives and daughters of heroes', and the mildly comic effect of a Don Juan is not intended.

Some of the gods who were assimilated to the sons and daughters of the Indo-European monogamous divine family had already mothers, if not fathers, of their own, and the former they retained after Zeus had taken

over their paternity. Similarly many heroes had a respectable pedigree ending in an ancestress, possible a mark of an earlier society in which a man might quite normally call himself Parthenius, 'unmarried woman's son'. But in most cases, paternity was taken over by a god. The god is often said to cast the maiden into a deep

sleep before possessing her, which might suggest some ritual use of drugs in a rite of sacred marriage to a god or in some cases to his representative.

The amours of Zeus thus reflect either ritual or genealogy or both. But in the monogamous Indo-European family a wife was not expected to tolerate her husband's concubines or

bastards, and when this social structure was projected upon heaven it produced a shrewish Hera.

Ares and Aphrodite
The legitimate issue of Zeus and Hera were in fact three, and only one of them is a member of the divine family. This is Ares, god of war, who

because he was lame. The male gods came, but the female ones stayed at home for shame. And Homeric laughter arose among them at the sight of the poetic justice by which the tortoise had caught the hare. Apollo said to Hermes, 'would you be willing, burdened with heavy chains, to sleep in a bed with golden Aphrodite? Hermes replied that he would not mind even if the goddesses looked on. But Poseidon was not amused, and called on Hephaestus to loose them, offering to stand surety for the fine that Ares would have to pay for his conduct. Ares went off to Thrace, but Aphrodite to Cyprus, to Paphos, where are her grove and altar, and there the Graces bathed her and anointed her with immortal oil and put on her lovely clothes, a wonder to see.

Athena

Hera and Poseidon are often associated with Athena as not overfriendly critics of Zeus. Athena, like Hera, is not a name but a title. It means 'the Athenian one' and refers to another manifestation of the pre-Greek mother-goddess worshipped, as she continued to be worshipped, in the Parthenon on the Acropolis at Athens. An Indo-European etymology for the name has, however, been suggested, meaning 'daughter of the father'. Athena was, however, quite literally absorbed by Zeus, who by pure thought brought her to birth from his forehead, fully armed in his own magic goat-skin, the aegis, though Hephaestus cleft his head with an axe to effect the delivery.

seems to have been in some way Thracian and to have presented to his sons savage maneating mares for their chariots. He appears in a famous story as the discomfited lover of Aphrodite.

Ares gave Aphrodite many gifts, and she shamed the bed of her lord Hephaestus. But the Sun, who sees everything, told him what was going on, and in anger he went to his forge and made chains like spiders' webs, quite invisible, which he hung from the bedposts as a kind of net, with a device for letting them down. Then he announced his intention of going off to Lemnos, the seat of his cult. He was no sooner out of the house than Ares was in, crying:

'Hither, dear, to the bed let us turn', a call to which Aphrodite responded with alacrity. Down came the net and back came Hephaestus, again warned by the Sun. In anger, he summoned father Zeus and the other gods, claiming that he was made a laughing stock by Aphrodite

Left. Bronze statue, perhaps of Poseidon. The 7-foot (213 cm) statue was recovered in 1928 from the sea off Artemisium, the cape on the north-western tip of Euboea where the Persians were defeated in a storm in 480 B.C. Presumably a treasure ship carrying art treasures to Rome was wrecked on the same treacherous coast. The statue is not Attic. It has been associated with the Aeginetan Onatas, who made the statue of Hermes with the ram at Olympia. The subject used to be taken as Zeus with the thunderbolt; now it is more frequently believed to be Poseidon with the trident. But the trident is used for stabbing (as in the coin of Paestum, bottom), and this statue appears rather to be hurling a spear. It might represent an idealised warrior rather than a god. National Archaeological Museum, Athens.

Below left. The birth of Athena was naturally a popular subject among Athenian vase painters. Some versions show Hephaestus cleaving the head of Zeus with an axe, but this, which belongs to a group E close to the master Exekias, and working about 560 B.C., shows Athena received into the family of Olympus despite her unorthodox birth. Zeus with a decorative thunderbolt sits on a stool, under which is a small sphinx, simply a space filler. To the left are Hermes and a bearded Apollo with the lyre. To the right are Ares dressed as a hoplite with Corinthian helmet fully on his head and a goddess who is perhaps Artemis, as Apollo's sister, or Aphrodite, Ares' lover. Museum of Fine Arts, Boston, Massachusetts. Pierce Fund.

Opposite. The seated figure of a goddess is a very old cult type: to remain seated being a mark of superiority before worshippers of smaller size who stand. In the late fourth century, in Asia Minor, the type was humanised, as in this great Demeter found there in 1858 and brought to the British Museum. Possibly the work of the sculptor Leochares, who worked on the great Mausoleum built by Mausolus for his wife and himself, it is perhaps the finest idealisation of the mother known from antiquity. Greek gods were always humanised from the time of Homer, and not always to their credit, but this statue shows the virtue of the approach. British Museum, London.

Left. Obverse of stater of Paestum, 530 B.C. The Italian town of Paestum was named after Poseidon and the Greek form of the name is Poseidonia. The god was always shown on the coinage together with the first three letters of his name reading upwards. He is almost always bearded, though that is not well indicated here. He holds the trident, a fishing spear, not to be thrown but for stabbing down into the water. Over his shoulders he wears what may be a net. British Museum, London.

Left. Persephone or Demeter. Big half figures, called protomes, were made in large quantities in Boeotia during the fifth century and placed in graves. An almost identical figure, possibly from the same mould, was found at Delphi where it may have been a dedication. The type is archaic, and may derive from a cult statue wearing the characteristic hat. The pose indicates a mother-goddess, holding a pomegranate bud in her left hand, either Persephone or Demeter as protectress of the dead. Museum of Fine Arts, Boston, Massachusetts. Perkins Collection.

Far left. Persephone and Hades. The Greek colony at Locri, on the toe of Italy, was the site of an important cult of Persephone. A large number of votive plaques all produced between 480 and 450 B.C. were found in a number of pits. All bear subjects related to the mysteries. Persephone is shown enthroned with Hades though she is clearly the more important figure. Museo Nazionale, Reggio, Calabria.

Left. Fertility goddess. This early-sixth-century statue from Megara Hyblaea in Sicily was painstakingly reconstructed from 936 fragments. It is a powerful representation of the fertility goddess who was, in one form or another, the chief deity of the Greek colonies in Sicily. Here the goddess is firmly maternal, and suckling twins. She is Demeter, therefore, rather than Persephone, although the twins may suggest a cult of Leto, mother of Apollo and Artemis. Museo Archeologico Nazionale, Syracuse.

Opposite. The Ludovisi Throne, named after the papal family on whose estates it was found, with its pair, the Boston Throne, is one of the most mysterious ancient works of art that have survived from the middle of the fifth century. It seems to have decorated an altar used in the cult of Persephone in southern Italy. Rejuvenation, or the triumph of love over age, is the theme of the reliefs. The relief shown seems to represent the Return of the Maiden, either from the sea, suggested by the pebbles on which the attendants stand, modestly veiling the lower limbs of the goddess, or from a ritual bath, or from the underworld. Museo Nazionale, Romano, Rome.

The story, as old as the *Theogony*, said that Zeus loved Metis ('counsel': a personification) but was warned by Earth that his son by her would supplant him and so he swallowed her. Athena was the child of this union. This is not the only myth in which Zeus appears in the role of Cronus. But the story of Athena's birth in fact reflects the resentment felt in a patriarchal society for woman's one indispensable function, actually bearing the legitimate children of the father. At least, they cry, the fathergod could have children by himself without the intervention of the mother. In human terms they devised the physiological theory that the child is complete in the male seed, and that the mother's contribution is no greater than that of the earth in which also they sowed seed. Psychologically, of course, Athena is the virginal and unmarried warrior daughter as typical of the Indo-European divine family as it may have been of the warrior society which that reflects.

Poseidon

Actual hostility between Poseidon, Hera and Athena on the one hand and Zeus on the other is found in the story of how Hera, Poseidon and Athena bound Zeus. Thetis the sea nymph released him and brought the hundred-handed Briareus, or Aegaeon, to help him. This story seems to bear traces of an alternative succession myth though some regard it as an Homeric invention to explain why Zeus owes Thetis a favour. Common to both is the presence of Briareus as Zeus' Helper, and there can be little doubt that Thetis is here standing for Tethys (the two are linguistic variants) who played in this alternative cosmology the role taken by Gaia in the standard version. It should follow that Ocean played the part taken by Uranus and if so Poseidon may stand for him here, and the binding for the hiding away of Uranus' children.

Certainly Poseidon seems to be the father of Briareus, who is here given an alternative name that links him with the Aegean Sea, and he may, like Atlas, have been the giant that stands in the sea and holds the world. If, then, in this version, Poseidon is Oceanus/Uranus, Zeus, who is never referred to by that name in it, must stand in the place of Cronus in what

was presumably a myth of single supplanting. As told in the *Iliad,* it is a tale of rivalry between the Olympian gods. But the terms in which it is told seem to go back to an older mythology.

Demeter

Like his titles, 'earth-holder, shaker of earth', the name of Poseidon points also to some such original role. It seems to mean 'Husband of Da' where Da, like Ge and Gaia, is a pre-Greek name of the mother-goddess Earth. Da reappears as the first syllable of Demeter, 'Da mother', who is in Greek religion the goddess of Agriculture and a sister of Zeus. Demeter had a daughter, Persephone by name but often called simply Koré, 'girl'. Zeus was her father, and exercising his paternal rights he gave her in marriage to Hades. Gaia approved the marriage and sent up flowers that tempted Persephone down a secluded valley which either led to Hades or where Hades raped her (flowers are the proper accompaniment of a sacred marriage, and Gaia had specially created the narcissus, which like Koré returns in

6570

the spring) and from where he carried her off.

Demeter heard the scream which her daughter gave, and sought her over the whole world, bearing the torches used in her ritual. In the shape of an old woman she came to Eleusis, and the king's daughters received her kindly, and brought her into the house to be nurse to their infant brother Demophoon. But in her sorrow she would not enter the house, but stood grieving until Iambe made her smile with obscene jests and set her on a chair. But she refused wine, asking instead for a gruel of flour and pennyroyal. She stayed and nursed Demophoon, anointing him with ambrosia and at night putting him in the fire, until one night his mother Metaneira caught her at it and struck her. So Metaneira lost the gift of immortality for her son, and Demeter continued her search for her daughter.

At last the Sun, who sees everything, told her what had happened, and Demeter went to Zeus and asked for her daughter back. Zeus was obliged to grant her wish, for in her grief and anger Demeter had witheld the kindly fruits of the earth, and mankind would have perished and the gods have lost their sacrifices. Nor would Demeter set foot upon Olympus at the feasts of the gods. So Zeus commanded Hades to send Persephone back to her mother, and Hades let her go with a smile; but he gave her a pomegranate seed to eat that she might be forced to stay with him a third of every year. Thus Persephone came up to Eleusis to join her mother. But Zeus called them to Olympus, promising them honours and bidding her make the earth fruitful once more. She despatched Triptolemus to teach men agriculture.

The myth arises out of the annual ritual of the Mysteries of the small and originally independent Attic town Eleusis, which were celebrated at the time of the autumn sowing. They involved a procession with torches, purification in the sea and probably also with pennyroyal, reci- tations, obscene jests, and rituals culminating in the revelation of something, perhaps an ear of corn. Demeter and the Girl are the two independent deities of these mysteries: the Girl is the seed corn which is hidden away in underground silos from June to October, when it is re-united with Mother-earth in the sowing. Triptolemus is a 'culture-hero' who travelled over the world in a car drawn by winged snakes teaching men the art of agriculture which he had learnt from Demeter. His name suggests the Tripolus, the 'thrice ploughed fallow' in which the corn was sown and where Demeter lay with another culture-hero Iasion, perhaps her original consort, in a rite to ensure the fertility of the crop.

Zeus is certainly an intruder in the myth and so perhaps is his shadowy brother Hades. One of the many euphemistic titles of Hades is Pluto, the rich one, probably at first a reference to the never-diminishing number of the dead: he is also called Polydeg-

Above. The sacred island of Delos, where the Ionians gathered together to hold a festival of Apollo on the island where he was born, lies to the south-west of Mykonos. The sacred site lay on the north-west coast of Delos, under the sacred mountain of Cythnus on which Zeus and Athena were worshipped. The ancient path up the mountain lay to the left of that prominent in the picture. To the north of the sanctuary was a sacred lake, just off the left of the picture, overlooked by a terrace of sacred lions, set up at the end of the seventh century by the Naxians, who dominated the island at that time.

Opposite. The cult of Demeter and her daughter, Koré, otherwise Persephone, was known in other places than Eleusis. These also laid claim to the culture-hero Triptolemus (perhaps he of the thrice ploughed furrow) who taught agriculture to the rest of the world. However, Athens claimed him early on together with agriculture as one of the great benefits the Athenians conferred on the world, and representations of his winged chariot are known in black-figure before the Persian Wars. In this red-figure vase by Makron, of the period of the Wars, Demeter on the left and Persephone on the right, each with the torches and corn ears of the ritual, send him on his way, providing him with a libation to pour before he sets out. British Museum, London.

mon, the receiver of many. But the son of Demeter and Iasion is also Plutus, wealth, again first in corn: there seems little trace in Greek of the idea that Hades is the source of gold and silver.

Since there already existed a goddess of the dead, Persephone, the assimilation of the two myths was easy. The descent of Koré was then equated with the sowing, and her reappearance with the coming of spring. On this, in the Hymn, has been superimposed the story of the provision of the bride for Hades: marriage with an uncle appears frequently in the myths and is connected with a system of inheritance. The wandering of Demeter in search of her daughter is then less well motivated, and she withholds the crops as a separate act of pique against Zeus, like her refusal to enter Olympus, which is hardly surprising in an originally pre-Olympian mother-goddess.

Leto, Apollo and Artemis

Another similar mother-goddess may have been Leto, who appears as daughter of two of the Titans. At any rate, she was the mother by Zeus of two of the gods, Apollo and Artemis, who are both archers and both in some way Eastern deities, though the Greeks assimilated Apollo to a wolf god of flocks and herds and his sister to a pre-Greek mistress of wild beasts. The connection of Apollo with Leto seems stronger: he is regularly called 'he whom fair haired Leto bore'. But he is also 'son of Zeus', a terrifying figure whose arrows cause plague and whose oracular shrine at Delphi proclaims the will of Zeus. His association with the Muses may have arisen there also, since they too can foretell the future, or may be an attribute of the shepherd god who plays the lyre. But singing and dancing also formed part of the cult of Apollo at Delos, his birth place.

Delos was the centre of the festival of all the Ionians of Asia Minor and the islands and was identified with Ortygia, the magic Quail Island on which Leto gave birth. A number of

27

folktale motifs, connected with the hostility of Hera to a rival, attached to the island. Leto was not to bring forth in any land that the sun had seen, and was pursued by the serpent of Delphi, the Python, which Apollo was to slay. In the *Hymn* it does not get this name until it rots, and is called Typhon, which Hera bore spontaneously with the help of Titans, in retaliation for the birth of Athena. This too is a piece of the old succession myth pressed into service.

Delos was at this time a floating island, into which Leto's sister had been turned when pursued in love by Zeus. Poseidon hid it beneath the waves, thus somehow making it fit Hera's conditions, and then fixed it where it now is. Ilithyia, the goddess of childbirth, was bribed with a necklace to desert Hera, for whom she was impeding the birth, and allow Apollo to be born. The goddesses washed the baby and Themis fed him on nectar and ambrosia to make him immortal. After this food he at once broke his swaddling clothes and almost his first action was to slay the Python and take over the oracular shrine of earth at Delphi, the second great centre of his cult. There his priestess, the Pythia, gave oracles in trance, associated with the Tripod, a bowl on three legs, on which she, or the god, was sometimes envisaged as sitting.

In one version the role of Ilithyia is taken by Artemis as soon as she is born. For Artemis too was invoked by women in childbirth, and though she is called Parthenos, 'un-married woman', was not perhaps originally virgin. In mythology she is associated with nymphs who become pregnant and are transformed into beasts. Their identity with Artemis is clearest in the story of Callisto: not only was Artemis called Calliste, 'fairest', but the nymph was seduced by Zeus in the form of Artemis, and was turned into a bear as punishment. In Brauron in Attica, where the sanctuary has recently been fully excavated, little girls in saffron dresses (worn also by prostitutes) impersonated bears in what seems to have been a kind of initiation into womanhood at puberty, in honour of Artemis. But Callisto was slain, either by Artemis, as on the coins of Arcadia, or by her own son, in punishment for violating a shrine of Zeus.

Both Artemis and Leto also are associated with giants. The first was Tityus, a son of Earth in the *Odyssey,* but also associated with Euboea where there was a cave named after his mother Elara and where he had a hero cult. Zeus was said to be his father, and he hid Elara in the earth to keep her from Hera. Tityus, who was 900 feet long, attempted to rape Leto, according to the myth in Delphi. Apollo and Artemis saved their mother by shooting Tityus with their arrows, and he is found in Hades being punished by two vultures, which sit either side of him and gnaw his liver. Another of the great sinners punished in Hades, Ixion, is also there for an attempt on a goddess, Hera.

But the birth and fate of Tityus strongly suggest the Titans, and his story seems to be another misplaced piece of a succession myth.

Orion

Even more curious is the story of the beautiful giant Orion, an earthborn child of Poseidon, who gave him the power of going through the sea, like Atlas and Briareus. In one version of his birth, Poseidon and other gods begot him (again without a woman) by making water on a hide, which was then buried for nine months. This is an example of folk-etymology (urine = Orion). Orion became a mighty Boeotian hunter, and had a wife

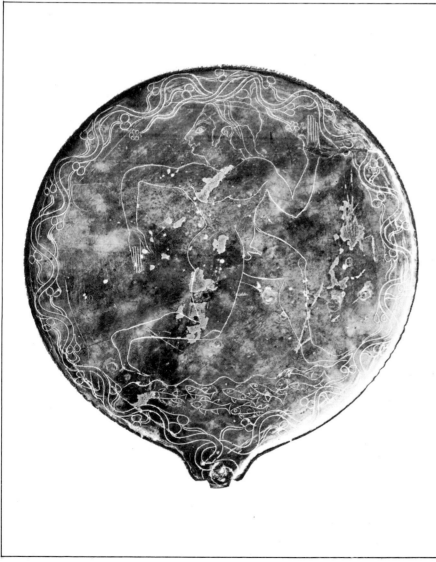

Left. Apollo and Artemis as helmeted archers, the former with the animal skin often worn by monster slayers, drive off the giant Tityus from their mother Leto whom he attempted to rape. Tityus, who is represented as 'wild man' with his body covered with hair, has been shot in the eye. Hermes, in winged boots, stands by, and for decorative purposes the artist has given the same boots to Apollo. The amphora is one of a group made in Athens in the early sixth century for the Etruscan market to cater for the taste there for vigorous and often gory scenes from mythology. Musée du Louvre, Paris.

Opposite right. Artemis and nymphs. Outside Athens there had been, at the very beginning of the sixth century, a technique of relief decoration of very large storage pots. From the neck of such a vase found and very likely made at Thebes comes this model of a goddess, clearly identified by the two lions who flank her and by the vine which grows from her head as the Mistress of Beasts, later identified with Artemis. The two female figures under her protection are therefore the nymphs of Artemis, though they give the goddess a very maternal appearance. National Archaeological Museum, Athens.

Opposite left. Obverse of stater from Croton, about 420 B.C. The Italian colony of Croton, at the western end of the gulf of Tarentum, was founded at the direct instance of Delphi, the clearing house for early Greek geographical knowledge, and so always showed the oracular tripod of Apollo on its coins. The tripod is ornamented with two twisted garlands, and on either side appear the infant Apollo and the coiled python which he shot when he took over the shrine from Earth. British Museum, London.

Opposite below. Artemis. This gold votive plaque from Rhodes of the seventh century B.C. shows oriental influences. The goddess is depicted winged, and with a head out of proportion to the body. The type is a variant of the Mistress of Wild Beasts, for here the lions have been tamed and overcome by the goddess. She is presumably Artemis, though the Mistress is a pre-Greek goddess. The hanging pomegranate flowers suggest that in Rhodes she retained some of the attributes of a fertility goddess. Ashmolean Museum, Oxford.

Left. Orion crossing the sea. Etruscan bronzeware was famous even in Greece, to which it may have been exported in exchange for Attic painted vases. Women were important in Etruscan society, which may account for the large production of finely decorated mirrors, from the sixth century onwards. An archaic example, perhaps from the late sixth century, shows a beautiful naked youth running across the sea, indicated by a shoal of fishes. The youth is Orion, the beautiful hunter, who has this special power. British Museum, London.

called 'Pomegranate' who was sent down to Hades for rivalling Hera, and may therefore have been a kind of local Persephone.

Then Orion went to Chios and wooed the daughter of Oenopion, the 'wine-faced', who made him drunk and blinded him, perhaps for raping her before marriage. Orion went perhaps to Lemnos, where he picked up, if Hephaestus did not give him, a boy, the original 'pigmy on the shoulder of a giant', who guided him to the sunrise, where he got back his sight. Orion rushed back to be revenged on Oenopion, who escaped him by hiding in a brazen house under the ground made by Hephaestus. Then Dawn loved him, and carried him to Delos, where Artemis slew him with her soft darts. Or it was Artemis whom he loved, or one of her nymphs.

There are a large number of primitive ritual elements in this story or stories, and many of them recur in other myths. Blinding is often a literary substitute for castration, and there seems little doubt that Orion was originally the male figure in a number of fertility rites, in some of which his female partner may have been originally Artemis. The stories of Orion are known only from allusions and late sources, so that the various elements in them cannot easily be disentangled in detail. But the water-walking giant where the sun rises is from a succession myth.

Otus and Ephialtes

Some of the characteristics of Orion are shared by Otus and Ephialtes, whose mother, a figure in the heroic genealogies, bore them to Poseidon. At nine years of age they were nine cubits broad and nine fathoms tall, and they tried to pile Ossa on Olympus and Pelium on Ossa to scale heaven. They were slain by Apollo, for they put Ares into a bronze jar, from which Hermes stole him. The object of their quest was, it seems, Hera and Artemis, and in less Apolline versions Artemis killed them herself; a hind ran between them at which they fired, and hit one another.

Otus and Ephialtes seem also to have been figures in a fertility cult, particularly associated with the island Naxos. They are sons of the threshing floor, or of a garden or vineyard (aloe) and their female partners seem to have been identified with Hera and Artemis. The manner of their death shows them to have been hunters, and perhaps to have met some ritual death which relieved everybody else of responsibility.

Right. The temple of Hephaestus at Athens is still popularly called the Theseum. It owes this name to the four metopes, two on each side at the east end, which depicted exploits of Theseus, and to an early assumption that the Athenians would have commemorated their great founder. But temples were built only to gods, and in fact the ten metopes of the east end showed ten labours of Heracles. The temple overlooked the market place, from which it was designed to be seen at its best and from where this photograph was taken. It stood by the quarter of the smiths and bronzeworkers, whose patrons were Hephaestus and Athena. Built about 449 B.C., it is the oldest temple built entirely of marble.

Opposite. This vase painting from the middle of the sixth century is close in style to that of the famous painter Exekias, though nowhere like his quality. It shows Dionysus, holding his vine and a cornucopia, supported on the left by Hermes and confronting a female with twins, one dressed, one nude, and a youth holding a frond of stylised vegetation, perhaps Ivy, which was used in the worship of Dionysus. If the figure is a goddess, one thinks, as did earlier scholars, of Leto with Apollo and Artemis. But the figure might be a mortal, whose twins indicate the general fertility induced by Dionysus and the horn of plenty he holds. British Museum, London.

Hephaestus

In one version of the myth of the birth of Apollo, Hera was said to have borne Typhon spontaneously in revenge for the birth of Athena. This story is more commonly told of Hephaestus, perhaps an eastern fire god who has been incorporated as an Olympian of the second generation and, if the Greeks did learn metal-working from the East, as the divine smith. As such, he is lame. For as a blind child can be apprenticed bard, so a lame one can work at the smithy, where he does not have to move about much and where the compensating overdevelopment of arms and shoulders is an advantage. The loss of an eye, from sparks, another occupational hazard of smiths, may be the origin of the one-eyed Cyclops.

In Homer, however, Hephaestus is the regular son of Zeus and Hera, just as perhaps Athena was the regular daughter. He was born lame, and a story is told in the *Iliad* how Hera cast him out of heaven and he was kept for a great year (eight years) by Thetis. The story has slightly sinister overtones, not only of exposure of unwanted children but also, as often where Thetis is concerned, of the primitive succession myth. It looks as if, in one version, Hephaestus was to be the god who overthrew Zeus: indeed, in a myth attested only on vase paintings, on which it was at one period extremely popular, one of the things that Hephaestus made during his absence was a magic throne with which he took his revenge. For Hera sat on it, and could not be released until Dionysus made Hephaestus drunk and persuaded him to return in triumph, riding on a donkey, in order to set free his mother.

Hermes

The last of the Homeric Olympians is Hermes: for Dionysus is not mentioned in either the *Iliad* or *Odyssey*, except for a very few allusions, and is in any case unique in having a mortal mother who comes in the heroic genealogies. Hermes' mother is Maia, a nymph, though her name 'mother' suggests a mother-goddess whose original young consort Hermes might have been. He sometimes appears as a god of the flocks of sheep, especially in Argos, where he stands in an intimate relation with the house of Atreus, and in Arcadia where he was born.

This association with the 'luck of the flocks' extended to all forms of luck, and Hermes was the god of all forms of magic and trickery, which the Greeks at first admired rather than condemned. Perhaps because

31

these were the characteristics especially of travelling men, or simply by identification with some other now unknown deity, Hermes was also the spirit of the piles of stones with which Greek travellers marked paths, boundaries and holy places. Shepherds use the mountain pastures that separate one city-state from another, and are acquainted with neighbouring shepherds, and are thus naturally used in early diplomatic exchanges, and their god, Hermes, becomes in this way the patron of heralds.

As a traveller and trickster, Hermes loved to accompany men, and to escort them. He used a magic rod to stupefy men while he practised magic and deception. He used it also on the special escort duty which he carried out as 'Psychopompus', the 'Conductor of Souls' to the underworld. When Hermes became the general herald and messenger of the gods the rod became his badge of office. He has this role already in the *Odyssey*; but in the *Iliad*, Iris, the rainbow, is the messenger of the gods.

But the sixth-century hexameter hymn to Hermes is concerned only with the first day in the life of this precocious trickster who

'born at dawn at midday played the lyre,
At evening he stole the oxen of far-shooting Apollo'.

Hermes was born in a cave on Mount Cyllene in Arcadia, where Zeus had visited his mother at night 'when sweet sleep held white-armed Hera', but left his cradle at noon already determined to seek the cattle of Apollo. At the threshold he found a tortoise, the shell of which, he saw at once, could be made into the sounding box of a lyre. So he went back into the cave and made the first lyre, on which he proceeded to sing of his own birth.

The theft of the cattle was thus postponed until the sun went down, the appropriate time: for Hermes had spent the afternoon planning sheer guile in his heart, the sort of things that men who are deceivers practise in the season of black night. He 'cut out' (a Greek metaphor as well) fifty of Apollo's cows from Pieria, where the god's cattle were stalled every night, and drove them backwards

over the sand to Triphylian Pylos in the neighbourhood of Olympia in the north-western Peloponnese, where the story may originally have been located. He himself improvised a kind of snow-shoe out of twigs, further to confuse his tracks or perhaps originally to make walking easier on soft sand. There he sacrificed two oxen, making fire by means of fire-sticks (perhaps another local story of the origin of fire), and hid away the rest. Then he went back to Cyllene and entered the cave through the keyhole in the form of a mist, and wrapped himself up again in swaddling clothes in the cradle.

He was thus able to claim, when Apollo taxed him with the theft next day, that he was not himself responsible, nor had he seen anybody else. Unsatisfied, Apollo haled him off to Olympus and accused him before Zeus, who of course knew the truth. But Hermes swore, quite correctly, that he had not driven the cows home, nor had he set foot on the threshold (which he had been at pains to avoid treading on). This concern for the literal truth of the oath, while encouraging an opponent to deceive himself by false inferences, is typical of an early state of society, and was much admired by the early Greeks. Zeus however reconciled the two gods: Hermes returned the cattle and gave Apollo the lyre and promised neither to steal his bow (as in some versions he had done already) nor to usurp his position as oracular mouth-

piece of Zeus. In return Apollo sent Hermes to his own elementary teachers of divination:

'For there are some Holy women,
    born sisters,
unmarried, rejoicing in swift wings,
    three:
on their heads they are sprinkled
    with white,
and they dwell in their houses under
    the fold of Parnassus
far off teachers of prophecy which
    as a herd boy
while still a child I practised.

The hymn to Hermes has indeed been interpreted sociologically as recording a reconciliation between the old established cult of Apollo, which grew in importance as the power of the Delphic oracle increased, and the newer cult of Hermes, which appealed to a lower social class in sixth-century Athens.

Pan

Whether or not that particular analysis is valid in this case, there can be no doubt that myths of different periods do reflect the changing status

Opposite top. The religious symbolism of south Italian terracotta plaques and figures is very mysterious, and this early-fifth-century plaque from Locri (about 470–460 B.C.) still awaits authoritative explanation. The figure on the right is certainly Hermes, in winged boots and travelling hat, shown as a severe bearded figure surely as the Escorter of Souls. The little chariot which he enters is drawn by young male and female figures, both perhaps winged, who have been identified as Eros and Psyche. One bears a bird, possibly a dove or a hen, and the other holds an ointment jar. Since Psyche is the soul, it seems likely that the plaque is in some way funerary. The central figure has been identified as Aphrodite, or at any rate the south Italian goddess of fertility and death who has some of her characteristics. Museo Nazionale, Taranto.

Opposite right. The wealth and power of Syracuse always enabled it to attract the best artists and writers of Greece and its coinage was always superb. After the defeat of the Athenian expedition to Syracuse in 412 B.C., some four drachma pieces were issued which seem to show Athena surrounded by the dolphins normal on Syracusan coins. The signature of the artist, Euaenetus, is on the helmet. The type can just possibly be explained as a variant of the normal Arethusa type, showing the Syracusan nymph helmeted to signify the threat and its defeat. The spring Arethusa was seen as a nymph who fled from the river Alpheus at Olympia in the Peloponnese. Alpheus pursued her under the sea and their waters mingled in a freshwater spring. British Museum, London.

Opposite left. The island of Peparethus off the coast of Thessaly just north of Euboea was famous in antiquity for its wine and oil. Both the vine and the olive flourish in poor soil and are spoiled by too much rain. The consequent prosperity seems to have enabled the inhabitants to strike a very good early coinage, and this running figure was used as an emblem at the beginning of the fifth century. It is probably a wind bearing garlands, perhaps Boreas the North-East wind which gave an easy run into the Thessalian gulf. Boreas was important for trade, but could also wreck ships on the treacherous lee shore of Euboea. British Museum, London.

Right. The tripod, a shallow bowl on three tall legs, played an important part in the ritual of the Delphic oracle, and, however improbable it may seem, the inspired priestess, the Pythia, was believed to squat on it to give her prophesies. So, in this watering pot by the Berlin painter, at his best in the period of the Persian Wars, a rather small Apollo is shown sitting with his lyre and bow on what is otherwise a rather large tripod. The wings indicate his journey over the sea (full of fishes and an octopus) to the Hyperboreans, the virtuous people who lived at the back of

the North wind: the dolphins perhaps allude to Dionysus, who took over the shrine in winter during Apollo's absence, and who is a favourite subject for this painter. Musei Vaticani.

of cults. The introduction of the cult of Pan at Athens, for example, is historically attested in a famous story which incidentally shows the reality of Greek faith in their myths. Before the battle of Marathon the Athenians despatched the runner Philippides to Sparta to ask for help. On the way he met Pan, who asked why the Athenians neglected him.

Pan, the 'Feeder' (of the flocks: the word is related to 'pasture'), is described in a *Hymn* as son of Hermes by the bride of the Arcadian Dryops, and as 'goatfooted, two-horned, noisy, laughing', which suggests that Hermes had assumed the form not of a mortal but a goat. Other Greek gods also assume in myth the form of animals or birds, and a three-tiered structure may be postulated, god and goddess, king and queen, animal and mate. Hybrids like Pan, centaurs and the Minotaur either reflect rationalistic confusion of the strata or the impersonation of the divine animal by the king. Pan seems in fact to be a more primitive form of that Arcadian god of the flocks who also evolved into Hermes. His form resembles that of the goat-satyrs who attended Dionysus and formed the chorus of the comic play that followed the three tragedies of an Athenian trilogy (the word 'tragedy' has been explained as 'goat song' – with some plausibility). But these goat-satyrs, like the horse-satyrs who are more common on vases, have human and not animal feet, perhaps because they are firmly derived from dancers impersonating animals.

Though in Elizabethan madrigals satyrs are always associated with nymphs, their proper prey is Maenads, the wild Bacchantes, followers of Dionysus over the hills taming snakes and tearing wild animals in their frenzy. Many Greek vases show Maenads fleeing from satyrs, repelling them with the thyrsus (a large pine cone set upon a stick of fennel) or, less commonly, yielding to them.

Nymphs

Pan on the other hand is associated with the nymphs, with whom he often shares a dedication, especially of a cave. These nymphs seem to be local manifestations of the early goddesses some of whom were upgraded into Olympians including Hera and Athena. Like Artemis, whom they continued to attend, they are creatures of the wild, and like her and Pan, they are dangerous to encounter. Pan causes irrational wild fear in the noonday silence of a deserted mountain side: the nymphs can cause madness, nympholepsy, which may also be prophetic inspiration.

The Greeks called brides 'nymphs', but whether this was because brides were held to be filled with some kind of divine power or because nymphs were supposed to be the brides of those they seized, is not clear. The inspired Pythia at Delphi, the various Sibyls, and even such unfortunates as Cassandra, were all regarded as in some sense 'brides of the god'. Nymphs were classified according to the natural objects with which they were associated: Oreads with the mountains, Meliae with ash groves, Dryads with those of other trees, especially oaks, Naiads with fresh water and Nereids, daughters of Nereus, with the sea. None of them are immortal, only, like the Sibyls, very long lived; how long is told in a Hesiodic fragment of traditional 'counting rhyme' form:

'Nine generations lives the
    chattering crow
as men grow old, the deer is four
    crows,
after three deers the raven grows
    old,
but the phoenix
lives nine ravens: and ten phoenixes
    we
nymphs with fine plaits,
daughters of aegis-bearing Zeus'.

In this passage the generation may mean a period of a hundred years, the Latin saeculum, the time of the longest human life, which would make the life of a nymph very nearly a hundred thousand years.

Even in this long life most nymphs were happy in having no mythological history. But Charon of Lampsacus, a fifth-century mythographer and historian, told a story perhaps in the course of his Persian history: A certain Rhoecus of Cnidos, being for some reason in Nineveh, saw an oak in danger of falling and bade his slaves to prop it up. Its Dryad appeared to him, thanked him for saving her life (which in this story is bound up with her tree), and offered him anything he liked to ask. He (of course) asked for her favours, which she promised him, and said that a bee should come to tell him when to visit her (there is a connection between

bees and nymphs already in the Odyssey, and some prophetic priestesses were called 'bees'). But when it came, Rhoecus was in the middle of a game of draughts and spoke to it rudely; whereat the offended Dryad blinded him. Whether she also gave him the gift of prophecy is not recorded in the fragment.

That was what happened to Tiresias, a nymph's son, though different stories are told to account for his blindness. Charon's story, attractive though it is, suggests a literary treatment of an original something like that of Cassandra in reverse, how a nymph granted Rhoecus the gift of prophecy, which she could not recall even when he spurned her favours. So she blinded him in revenge.

The Greek cosmogony with which the previous section was concerned is, at least in the literary form which alone survives and which was quoted there, at least as much of a deliberate piece of story telling as that of Charon, and some of its sources can be pointed to with some degree of certainty. The process of myth making is always the same: the spirit in which it is done, however, varies greatly.

The author of the Theogony claimed a high moral purpose: in his language, he was inspired by the Muses. He told his myths seriously and they can be shown to have satisfied deep psychological needs in himself and in his hearers. Charon of Lampsacus seems to be more of an entertainer, telling the sort of marvellous and romantic story that his audience liked to hear. He may, like his younger contemporary Herodotus, have possessed a firm faith in 'the divine': but he is not committed to his stories, which got for 'the mythological' the bad reputation that led Thucydides to expel it explicitly from his scientific history. A great many Greek myths, unfortunately, survive only in versions which have been subjected to this kind of romantic embellishment which began as early as the fifth century, even though it is especially typical of learned Alexandrian poetry.

Early Man

There does not seem to have been any canonical story of the creation of man in Greek mythology. There is a late tradition in Greek mythology that Prometheus made man out of clay, into which Athena breathed life and spirit, and this is rather doubtfully attributed to Hesiod. The earlier Greeks seem simply to have supposed that men, like plants and animals, arose spontaneously from the earth. Such 'earth-born' men are said to have founded many dynasties – all those in fact of which the heroic genealogy did not start with a god, and even in cases when it did the mortal mother sometimes belongs to such an 'earth-born' family.

The Five Ages

But Hesiod systematised these races of men in a moral fable. His story of the Five Ages of Men is really part of his reaction to the hard times in which he found himself, combined with the common observation of the elderly that sons are not half the men their fathers were. He imagines a steady degeneration in terms of the four metals in common use, gold, silver, bronze and iron. This scheme was at first purely symbolic: Hesiod knew himself to be living in the age of Iron because mens' hearts were hard as iron. He knew too that he was living in a guilt culture: for in this age, he says, Aidos and Nemesis left earth. Aidos, the shame that a man feels before the disapproval of his peer group, and Nemesis, the righteous indignation of this group, are the forces preserving morality in a shame culture. As the authority of the peer group breaks down in different social conditions, there are no moral restraints on the actions of the strong until the Super-ego has been 'internalised' as conscience, the moral sanction of a guilt culture.

But Hesiod was also living in an age that habitually used iron for tools and weapons, but which knew itself to have succeeded an age in which bronze was used at least for the latter. The bronze men, however, were already degenerate, and notorious for their violence. Though this may appear a fair, if harsh, description of the Homeric heroes, it would not do for Hesiod, for whom these were juster and better than his contemporaries. So he interrupted his scheme of generations, and interposed them as a fourth race between the bronze and the iron.

The first race, then, that the immortals made was of gold. They were in the time of Cronus, and they lived like gods, without labour and pain. They did not suffer from old age, but died as if falling asleep, and the earth bore fruit for them of her own accord in ungrudging quantity. Now that the earth has hidden this race they are spirits, good ones under the earth, guardians of mortal men and givers of wealth.

It is tempting for those who know the rich golden hoards of the Mycenean shaft graves (from about 1600 B.C. onwards) to see here some memory of this period, since one of the tombs has a structure which has been taken as meant for libations. But the belief in a past golden age, Virgil's 'reign of Saturn', who was identified with Cronus, may be explained largely as a compensation fantasy for the hard times of the present period.

The second race was of silver. They were far worse than the golden race, quite unlike them in form and mind. None the less they were long lived: a child was suckled for a hundred

years. But when they were fully grown their life was short: for in wanton violence they could not keep their hands off each other, and refused to worship the gods or do them sacrifice. So Zeus hid them in his wrath. None the less they too are called 'blessed ones under the earth', second-class it is true, but they receive continuous honours. It seems likely that in both these cases there is a reference to the earth burials of these earlier Greek cultures: in Homer and in Hesiod cremation was the rule, and the dead are witless and twittering ghosts and never the objects of cult, which was reserved for these buried heroes.

The third race of bronze men were in fact made out of the ash stems which provided their spears but their houses, arms and tools were bronze. Nor did they eat corn, but their stout minds were of adamant, and strong and violent they slew one another and went down to the mouldy hall of dank Hades, nameless. They were then the object of no cult: but their

eating habits reflect the great shift that took place between heroic and classical Greece. The Homeric heroes were meat eaters, as befits a cattle-breeding aristocracy: Homeric banquets are of 'meats in profusion and sweet drink'. Classical Greeks ate bread as a staple with olives, cheese, pickled fish and garlic to make it go down.

Homeric heroes themselves are for Hesiod the intrusive fourth race of men, who died in war, some at Thebes fighting for the sheep of Oedipus, and some at Troy. At their death they went to the Isles of the Blest, the golden age all over again now located far off in space not in time.

'Never', then cries Hesiod, 'ought I
  to have been among the fifth men
but either die before or be born
  afterwards,
for now is the race of iron, when
  never by day
they cease from toil and woe, nor by
  night from being worn'.

But his chief concern is not for cares and labour, but for the injustice that divides family and has led to the departure of Shame and Indignation. Earlier he had told a different myth to account not for the injustice of the world but for its evils. Chief among these, for Hesiod, is work.

Prometheus
Zeus limited the fruitfulness of the earth, angry because he had been cheated by the Titan Prometheus, son of Iapetus and brother of Atlas. Like Atlas he is eventually punished by being shackled to a mountain in the Caucasus while his liver is gnawed by an eagle. He is thus one of the giants whose tortured writhings cause earthquakes. But the Greeks very early took his name to mean 'Forethought' and gave him a brother 'Afterthought', Epimetheus, and in many respects he behaves like the first man, Clever, with his brother Foolish. How, as such, he cheated Zeus is told in the *Theogony*.

Formerly men and gods ate together (and specially favoured mortals such as Tantalus continued to be admitted to the feasts of the gods). But when they were separated, Prometheus slaughtered a great ox, and divided it into two heaps. In one he put the meat and the offal inside the hide, covering it with the stomach and intestines, so that it looked a nasty small heap. But he made a pile of the bones and covered them with the fat, a great big heap. Zeus complained the two heaps were not the same size, so Prometheus generously let him choose which he would have. Deceived, Zeus chose the larger. From that time men burnt on the altars of the gods the fat and the bones, and the rest they kept for themselves.

Hesiod of course claims that Zeus was not really deceived, and that his wrath was excited by the intention to deceive. This sophistication shows that the story is older than Hesiod: but he is right in seeing that the story explains the sacrificial ritual of his day. It is an aetiological myth. The real reason why the fat and the bones were burnt was that sacrifice was originally a sacred meal at which men either ate the god in the form of his sacred animal, or shared a meal with the god who was believed to be present. They consumed or used all the useful parts of the animal: the rest was burnt because it was holy. When the gods were conceived of as living up in heaven, they were believed to take pleasure in the sweet savour of a burnt offering, and indeed to live off the smoke. The holocaust was introduced, at which the whole victim was burnt for the god, and it became necessary to explain why, in the regular sacrifice, the gods were given the worse part. The folk tale motif of the Trickster was invoked, and the deceit takes its place in the complicated story of how the world came to be the way it is.

For in retaliation Zeus either hid fire away or witheld it from the ash trees from which men extract it by fire sticks, which they rub together until the hidden fire is revealed. But Prometheus, like a good culture hero, stole it from heaven where it can be seen in sun and stars, and from which it descends in lightning. He carried it away, as men did, in the hollow stem of a dried fennel, stopped up with clay at either end so that the pith should not smoulder away too quickly.

Pandora

But Zeus still had a trick in hand. He had Hephaestus make a clay figure like a maiden, equipped with all kinds of monstrous guile, and Athena dressed her, and Zeus gave her to foolish Epimetheus, who accepted her. For the poet of the *Theogony*, in the tradition of Greek misogyny, there is no greater evil than the race of women, who are like drones in the hive, consuming a man's substance. But you cannot cheat Zeus: for there is one thing worse than a wife, and that is not having one. For then you have no children to look after your old age, and your relatives, and not your sons, divide your inheritance when you are dead.

Hesiod, in the *Works and Days*, says that the woman was named Pandora, and Epimetheus accepted her although Prometheus had warned him to accept no gifts from Zeus.

The name Pandora, which Hesiod explains by the gifts with which she was endowed, shows the story is based upon religious ritual. For Pandora is the Giver of All, that is, the Earth goddess, and a vase painting, as so often, preserves a different and perhaps a more primitive form of the myth. It shows Epimetheus, armed with a hammer or possibly a double axe, releasing from some kind of underground chamber a Pandora who is rising from the earth. This motif, which suggests the return of Persephone, recurs in, among other places, the *Peace,* of Aristophanes, where the hero Trygaeus, the man of the Vintage, releases Peace from the subterranean chamber in which War has imprisoned her, and thereby regains his youth.

This suggests that Pandora was once a blessing rather than an evil, whose return released men from the starvation to which they were reduced. Indeed Hesiod goes on to tell the well known story by which Pandora was not herself the evil, but simply the cause by which evils came upon the earth, admittedly through her feminine curiosity. For Epimetheus had, or Pandora brought with her, a great storage jar, like those found in Cnossus, in which were all the evils that might attack man. Presumably Zeus, benevolent in this version, had bottled them up and men were still living in the Golden Age. But Woman took out the bung, just as the companions of Odysseus undid the goat-skin which held all the contrary winds, and out they all got. But Hope clung to the lip of the jar and did not get out, for the woman put back the bung before she could get out. Hope was not always regarded as a blessing by the Greeks: for while desire pushes them from behind, it leads them on from in front to commit acts of folly. But the point of view may have shifted rapidly, as is possible in myths, and the traditional explanation may be right, that Hope has stayed with men and alone reconciles them to their evil plight. Diseases originally had voices and gave audible warning of their approach, so that men could avoid them. But now Zeus, angry for some reason with men, has taken away their voices, and they can attack men without warning by day and night.

Deucalion

The mythical chronology of these tales of the creation of man is quite uncertain and inconsistent. For Pandora is clearly supposed to be the first

A vase in the severe classical style of about 450 B.C. depicting a ritual version of the myth of Pandora. She rises from the earth to be the bride of Epimetheus, as a Love hovers over her. Epimetheus' hammer is not a smith's hammer but the type that might be used to break open a prison or to break clods of earth. Hermes, as a young man with all his attributes including the winged hat, brings a flower from Zeus, perhaps to symbolise the charms of Pandora, but appropriate too if she is the returning spring. It is hardly a charm, as was the flower moly which Hermes gave to Odysseus to protect him from the wiles of Circe. Ashmolean Museum, Oxford.

woman, and yet men already existed in the reign of Cronus. But at this stage they join on to the heroic genealogies of the Greeks. For the daughter of Epimetheus and Pandora is said to be Pyrrha, who was the wife of Deucalion, 'the Greek Noah' who alone survived the flood with which Zeus destroyed the men of bronze. They re-peopled the earth by throwing over their shoulders the bones of their mother, that is, the stones of the earth, which became men and women according to whether Deucalion or Pyrrha threw them. The stones are folk etymology, since the Greek word resembles that for people (*laas* and *laos*).

The flood is variously motivated. Some ingeniously connected it with the fate of Phaethon, the 'sorcerer's apprentice', who begged to drive the chariot of his father the sun, but, failing to control it, plunged to his death: his mourning sisters were turned into poplars dripping amber tears into the Po, the southern end of the over-land amber route from the Baltic. In the course of his erratic career Phaethon came too near the earth, and besides, presumably, turning the negroes black, he set it on fire. This gave Zeus the excuse to destroy the bronze men by deluging the earth with rain under the pretext of putting out the fire started by Phaethon.

Lycaon

Others said that the flood was occasioned by the impiety of Lycaon, king of Arcadia, which was then called Pelasgia after Lycaon's father, the earth-born Pelasgus. 'The men of those days', Pausanias says, 'were guests and shared the same table with the gods for their justice and piety, and they openly met at the gods' hands with honour, those who were good, and those who had done wrong similarly with wrath'. But then Zeus visited the Arcadians in the guise of a work-man, and wanting to test whether it really was Zeus, either Lycaon or his fifty sons mixed with the flesh of the sacrifice the entrails of a baby. This so angered Zeus that he turned Lycaon into a wolf, overturned the table at the place named

after it Trapezus, and blasted with thunderbolts the sons of Lycaon, all but the youngest, Nyctimus, who was saved when Earth caught hold of Zeus' right hand and appeased him. Then he overwhelmed the earth with rain.

This is another aetiological myth, explaining the gruesome ceremonies which survived on Mount Lycaeus apparently to the time of Pausanias, who says that they sacrificed there in secret to Lycaean Zeus, but 'officiously to pry into the rites of the sacrifice was not to my taste: let it be as it is and has been from the beginning'. It was believed that ever since then, one man at the sacrifice turned into a wolf, and remained in that form for nine years or for ever if during that period he tasted human flesh. The were-wolf was probably the man who ate at the sacrifice the portion that had in it the baby's entrails, and he may have become the wolf-priest of Zeus until the next sacrifice, when, unless the distribution was fixed, he might be lucky enough to hand over the post to a successor.

The priest was in fact a rain-maker: for there was a spring on Mount Lycaeus which flowed in summer as well as winter (which is not true of all springs in Greece). When there was a drought, the priest agitated the surface of this spring with an oak branch, whereupon a mist arose, which turned into a cloud, which attracted others and brought rain to Arcadia. It is not surprising, therefore, that Lycaon's sacrifice produced a flood.

The poor and inhospitable hills of Arcadia were always the most primitive part of Greece. There are many primitive survivals in the myth and the ceremony, which may have started as the regular sacrifice and ritual cannibalism of a sacred king impersonating the god: later he invested his son with the sovereignty and sacrificed him (as the baby sacrificed by Lycaon is sometimes said to have been his son), ultimately to be succeeded by the youngest son of his mother. Eventually the sacred kingship was down-graded to a priesthood, and an unwanted baby

substituted for the sacrifice. There are many traces of this type of ritual in other Greek myths, which will be noted in their place.

The Flood

Deucalion, however, lived in Phthia, in Thessaly, where the original Hellas was and which has some claims to be the original home of many Greek traditions. When the rains came, Deucalion was advised by his father Prometheus to build a chest in which he floated for nine days and nights (perhaps originally years, another great year) before landing on the top of Mount Parnassus which was apparently never submerged and to which the inhabitants of Lycoreia, 'Wolf Mountain', claimed to have been led to safety by the howling of (sacred?) wolves. Similarly the Megarians claimed that their founder Megarus, son of Zeus and a local Sithnid water-nymph, had been led to the summit of the nearest mountain by the cry of cranes. Others brought the chest to rest on a mountain in Thessaly, perhaps the original site, on Mount Athos, or even on Mount Etna in Sicily. But the fame of Delphi and Parnassus naturally made it the canonical site.

The motif of escape in a floating chest recurs in the myth of Perseus and Danae, and might reflect a ritual way of avoiding sacrifice. There seem to be some relics of rain magic in the story of the flood. Flood myths are not, however, confined to Greece, and though they may also be memories of real local inundations, such as the famous one that buried Ur under twelve feet of silt, they may equally reflect the infantile fantasies of the child learning bladder control, who fears that he may drown the world in an uncontrollable flood, and his relief when he realises that the world has been delivered from this awful fate. As always, the myth can be explained in different terms at different levels.

The descent of Athamas, the son of Aeolus, the son of Hellen, the son of Deucalion and Pyrrha, shows how these timeless creation myths join on to the heroic genealogies of the Greeks, dealt with next.

The Children of Io

Genealogical interest is typical of very many primitive societies, and important questions of status, precedence and property ownership may depend upon the accurate establishment of descent. The Maori chiefs of the end of the nineteenth century could recite their pedigrees, apparently quite accurately, right back to the Polynesian invasion of New Zealand. Attempts have been made to try to establish a genealogical chronology of the pre-Dorian period by using the Homeric pedigrees.

But these pedigrees were not only preserved in the metrical formulae of hexameter poetry; they were also continued into the historic period. For many royal and noble families in Greece and Asia Minor traced their descent from Homeric heroes on both the Greek and Trojan side. Aeneas is twice rescued in battle by the gods, once by Aphrodite from Diomede and once from Achilles by Poseidon. In the first case Aphrodite substitutes an image of him to be fought over, which suggests that he may have been killed in the original tradition. But in the second Poseidon gives an explicit motive for his intervention, 'that the race of Dardanus might not perish to destruction without seed: for Cronides loved him above all his other sons. Now the might of Aeneas shall lord it over the Trojans, and so shall his children's children, who shall come after him'.

There were then kings or nobles in the neighbourhood of Troy who claimed descent from Aeneas, and for this reason (they were perhaps potential patrons of epic poetry) Aeneas had to survive the fighting at Troy and its fall. It was his survival which made him such a convenient ancestor for all those doubtfully Greek cities on the way to Italy, where he was already known in the fifth century, and ultimately for the Romans when they wished, perhaps after defeating Pyrrhus, who could claim descent from Achilles, to establish their standing among the Greeks with a heroic ancestor.

Systematised catalogues were characteristic of Boeotian poetry. A similar process was carried out for the heroes in the sixth and fifth centuries, when the social prerogatives of aristocratic birth were being challenged. These logographers, as they are called to distinguish them from the surviving and respectable historians Herodotus and Thucydides, started the practice of filling out a genealogy by turning places and tribes into people, and did their best to establish a consistent relation between different mythological figures. But the poets and dramatists still felt quite free to invent their own traditions, and there are, for example, several quite different accounts of the fate of Haemon and Antigone.

The Alexandrian scholars contin-

ued the work of systematisation, and
on the basis of their efforts Eratos-
thenes calculated the date of the Sack
of Troy as the equivalent of 1184 B.C.
This Alexandrian scholarship lies behind the extensive genealogies in
Apollodorus. But complete consist-
ency was never obtained: variants
and contradictions abounded, and
loose ends were left. That is why the
emperor Tiberius could quite
seriously ask his scholarly friends, the
Greek 'grammarians' 'Who was Hecuba's mother?' and 'What song the
Sirens sang, or what name Achilles
assumed when he hid himself among
the women?'.

Some genealogies went very far

back and are linked with the two
great centres of Mycenaean Greece,
Boeotian Thebes and Argive Mycenae. Both Cadmus, founder of
Thebes, and Danaus, who became
ruler of Argos (the foundation of Mycenae was reserved for a descendant,
Perseus), are represented as immi-
grants from Phoenicia and Egypt respectively. But both are provided with
quite respectable Greek antecedents
through their great common ancestress Io, and Danaus is certainly the
eponym of the Danaans, a tribe who
have provided another name for the
Greeks in the *Iliad* and also used to
be found in the Egyptian inscription
of Ramases III in 1186.

Io

Io was priestess at the Heraeum, the
famous and ancient shrine of Hera at
Argos, being the daughter of the local
river Inachus (though she was also
provided with a long artificial genealogy which gave eponyms and a history to many of the places in the
whole Peloponnese). Zeus loved her,
and she was turned into a heifer,
either by Zeus, to conceal her from
Hera after he had lain with her in the
form of a cloud or had covered the
place with a cloud to hide this sacred
marriage of Sky-father and Earth-
mother, or by Hera, to keep her from
Zeus, who therefore assumed the
form of a bull.

At some stage Io was tethered to an olive tree in the grove of the Mycenaeans and guarded by the All-seeing Argus, who himself wore a bull's hide and had eyes all over his body, and (in some versions) two faces. Zeus, in the form of a hawk or a woodpecker, guided Hermes to the spot. Hermes charmed Argus, with the music of the pipe though perhaps originally with his magic rod, and stole Io away from Argus, whom he slew with the cast of a stone. Then Hera sent a gadfly which drove Io by a circuitous route to Egypt. In Egypt she bore her son and called him Epaphus, either because by a touch (which is what the word means) Zeus restored her to her real shape, or because she had conceived simply at a touch.

Almost all the amours of Zeus reflect ritual as well as genealogy and it is not difficult to see how the myth of Io could be explained in terms of the ritual of the Argive Heraeum. There are clear traces in myth of a bull cult of Zeus, who assumed that form to abduct Europa, and of the identification of Io with Hera herself, who retains in Homer the traditional epithet normally translated as 'ox-eyed' but probably originally meaning 'cow-faced'. The mating of the sacred bull to a sacred heifer might lie behind the myth, and might have been preceded by the ritual slaughter of the new bull's predecessor, who turns up as Argus in his bull hide.

Nothing of this, of course, was known to any of the Greek narrators of the developed myth, who simply repeated the traditional elements in any order that suited them, and included elements from other rituals. Some Mycenaean monuments suggest that they visualised the descent of a god as a bird. The gods in Homer frequently appear and disappear in this form, and there was a legend that Zeus himself seduced Hera first in the form of a bedraggled cuckoo, as he did Leda in the form of a swan.

This then explains the appearance of Zeus in the form of a bird. Hermes is made to kill Argus, rather than exercise his traditional craftiness, to explain his title Argeiphontes, which may really mean 'slayer of Argus', though not necessarily originally of *this* Argus.

The Egyptian connection has sometimes been taken seriously, and very early Greek contacts with Egypt have been thought to be implied by the Homeric references to Egyptian Thebes, which ceased to be the capital of Egypt in about 1400 B.C. More probably at some stage the Greeks were impressed by the Egyptian bull cult of Apis, and the cow goddess Isis, with whom they identified Io. Her son Epaphus provided ancestors for many of the eastern nations. His daughter Libya bore twins to Poseidon: of these Agenor went to Phoenicia and Belus (Ba'al) married a daughter of the Nile and also begot twins, Egyptus and Danaus.

Human twins have always excited superstition, and in some parts of England used to be taken as proof of a wife's infidelity. In Greece the second husband implied in this view was taken to be a god, and one of the pair is sometimes mortal: alternatively, only a god is strong enough to beget two sons at once. Twins therefore occur very frequently in Greek mythology: not all of them have divine parents, for some may reflect the institution of dual kingship which survived at Sparta in the historical period.

Dual kingship may have been a device for reconciling two systems of inheritance. Two brothers marry two unrelated heiresses, each thus acquiring title to a kingdom in the female line. In each succeeding generation the son of one house marries the daughter of the other, so that the kingdoms are exchanged regularly, but each grandfather is succeeded by his grandson in the male line. This grandson often appears in the stories, somewhat inconsistently, as his daughter's son, though by strict matrilinear succession he should be the granddaughter's husband. This hypothesis (for that is all it is) has the merit of providing a single simple explanation for a number of the more puzzling structural features of these stories, though the whole pattern is rarely if ever found in any one myth.

The Daughters of Danaus

Danaus and Egyptus had each the traditional fifty children, Egyptus sons and Danaus daughters. A marriage was proposed between the two, but either Danaus or his daughters rejected it and fled to Argos, where the Argives accepted Danaus as king after Apollo sent a wolf to kill an

Argive bull as an omen. The sons of Egyptus pursued their brides across the sea, and Danaus feigned consent to the marriage, but ordered his daughters to kill their husbands on the marriage night and bring him their heads, which he buried separately. Then he found his daughters husbands by giving them away as prizes in a foot-race. But after their death these Danaids were punished in Hades: they had to carry water in sieves to fill a leaking pot. But one Danaid refused to kill her husband, Lynceus, who eventually became king after Danaus.

A number of recurrent motifs appear for the first time in this story, though not very clearly, together with some motifs that are peculiar to it. The Greeks did not believe in punishment after death until the time of Plato, except for a few notable sinners, including the Danaids. But the form of their punishment suggests that they were originally spring-nymphs, or priestesses with magical powers for finding springs. One of them, Amymone, appears as exercising just that power. When Poseidon and Hera contended for the land of Argos, Inachus adjudged it to Hera, and Poseidon in anger dried up all the springs. Danaus sent Amymone to draw water on their arrival. She occupied her search by hunting, and throwing at a deer hit a sleeping satyr. Poseidon saved her from the satyr's advances, only to press on her his own. In return, he revealed to her the perennial springs of Lerna, important in the summer drought of Greece.

A similar contest between Poseidon and the mother-goddess of the land is reported for Attica: there too Poseidon created a spring on the Acropolis, but of salt water. The well sounded like the sea when the south-west wind blew and there was the mark of a trident on a near-by rock. But Athena created the olive and was awarded the land. These contests may legitimately be taken to reflect conflict between the patriarchal religion of the Greeks and earlier mother-goddesses.

It is clear that Danaus and his daughters were opposed to their marriage with their 'parallel' cousins, (their father's brother's sons); such a marriage does not increase the number of kin (an important motive for marriage) as does the approved marriage to a 'cross-cousin' (a father's sister's son), who belongs to a different patrilinear family. Or it may be a reminiscence of Egyptian brother-sister marriage, of which the Greeks did disapprove. But perhaps it was marriage and not children that the Danaids objected to, and perhaps they killed their husbands after intercourse and not to preserve their virginity. The suggestion that Danaus quarrelled with Egyptus over the kingdom is the transference of a common motif in the history of twins, but cannot provide sufficient motivation. A similar motif is the foot-race for brides: there is normally only one winner who supplants his father-in-law, the situation of Hypermnestra and Lynceus. Elements in their story were connected with landmarks in Argos and with various rituals. The separate burial of the heads may simply be a device to account for the existence of two separate 'tombs of the suitors'. Or it might be magic, to lay their ghosts or to protect the land.

Danaus then was linked with Argos in this way, like his great ancestress Io. The other branch of Io's descendants was brought to Crete and to Thebes, and retained the bull cult which in Argos seems to have been superseded by that of the wolf god Apollo Lyceius, whose intervention secured Danaus the kingdom. Agenor became king of Tyre, where Europa and Cadmus were either his children or grand-children. Zeus loved Europa, and came for her in the form of a bull, carrying her off to Crete where a bull cult is copiously illustrated. The monuments seem to show bull-leaping, but this may be a euphemistic way of referring to goring. The name Europa, 'broad-faced', is quite appropriate for a cow.

Cadmus

Cadmus, with his mother and brothers, set out to look for Europa, and settled in various places to which they gave their names. Cadmus himself followed a cow, later said to be marked on the flank with a moon, until it lay down: there he founded a city – the Cadmea, the citadel of the later Thebes. The Delphic oracle claimed that he was following its advice: but the Italic *ver sacrum*, or sacred spring, provides a close parallel. This was a device for dealing with over-population in the poor but empty hill country of central Italy. Every so often all the live births, human and animal, of a year were vowed to the god. When they came to maturity, they went out to found a new tribe, following an ox or other sacred animal, which they sacrificed at the new tribal centre, which was therefore called Bovianum, 'Oxton'. One of the Greek tribes that came to Thebes seems to have followed the same custom, and it is the cow which has led to the association with Europa.

Cadmus himself was associated with snakes and with Ares. The spring on the Cadmea was sacred to Ares, and, as such springs often are, was guarded by a snake (not a dragon: the Greek *dracon* is fierce and mythical but still a snake). Cadmus killed it and sowed its teeth in the earth, from which armed men sprang up, who fell to fighting, either spontaneously or when Cadmus cast a stone among them. Five survived, the ancestors of the Theban aristocracy, who called themselves Sparti, 'sown men', and clearly prided themselves on being autochthonous, earth born. Cadmus served Ares for a great year to atone for killing his snake, or possibly to win his daughter Harmonia. For Cadmus, like Peleus, is

Opposite. Europa and the bull. The city of Selinus in Sicily was finally sacked in 409 B.C. by the Carthaginians, in support of Segesta, another Sicilian settlement. They hastily repaired the fortifications, destroying an old mid-sixth century limestone temple to provide stone. A metope, which was recovered almost undamaged, shows Zeus, in the form of a bull, carrying off Europa to Crete over a sea symbolised by dolphins. Museo Nazionale, Palermo.

The Birth of Dionysus

Ino also has Thessalian connections, for she married Athamas, one of the sons of Aeolus, with whom her fate was linked. The story of the other two sisters is that of the god Dionysus. Semele is his mother: but she was not originally the daughter of Cadmus, for her name is that of the Phrygian earth-mother, Zemelo, and she is one of the Phrygian elements in the cult of an originally Thracian god. Agave was the mother, by one of the sown men, of Pentheus, whose name seems to mean 'man of sorrows'. For his opposition to the Bacchic worship of Dionysus he suffered the fate of being ritually torn to pieces by Maenads, which was once the fate of the god whose substitute or surrogate he is. For Dionysus is the blend of the Thracian and Phrygian gods of vegetation and fertility, who were ritually torn to pieces by their worshippers in the form of a man, a bull or a goat. Impersonation, of the god or his sacred animals, was part of the ritual and the germ of drama.

The Phrygian god was particularly the god of the vine: for wine induces the ecstatic sense of release which was experienced by the worshippers of Dionysus, and which led to the rapid spread of the cult, especially among women. It compensated for the hard times and social tensions of the guilt culture of the dark ages of Greece after the end of Mycenaean culture. The Mycenaeans did apparently know a god called Dionysus, but the rapid expansion of his ecstatic cult was almost certainly later, and his peculiar divine status is reflected in the fact that he is the only one of the Olympians who is said to have been born of a mortal woman.

All Greek gods were born: but it is almost the definition of Greek divinity that the gods are ageless and immortal, all that men would wish themselves to be. A 'dying god', perfectly at home in Thrace or Phrygia, was a theological impossibility in Greece. So the myths of Dionysus are full of human surrogates whose stories and those of other dying heroes were enacted in his honour at the dramatic festivals of Athens.

one of the mortals who is allowed a goddess for a wife, and whose wedding the gods attended.

Harmonia is one of the attendants on Aphrodite like Hebe ('youth'), the Hours (actually plural of *Horé*, season of spring or youth) and Graces. Harmonia came with a divine dowry, a robe and a necklace, the latter made by Hephaestus and containing irresistible love-charms. Like the golden apple 'for the fairest', which appeared at the wedding of Peleus and Thetis, it did not bring good luck. At the end of their lives Cadmus and Harmonia left Thebes and led a tribe called Eel-men to victory against the Illyrians, of whom they became the king and queen, being turned into great serpents. That is to say they were identified, probably not before the time of Euripides, with the snake gods of an Illyrian tribe. In fact, as deified ancestors, they received offerings as snakes, very likely in Thebes itself.

The Daughters of Cadmus

Only Cadmus' daughters appear in the stories of the next generation at Thebes. Their names were Autonoe, Ino, Semele and Agave. Autonoe married Aristaeus, a rustic deity who presides over bee-keeping and olive-growing and sends forty days of cooling winds in the summer. He was the son of a Thessalian huntress, whom Apollo loved when he saw her wrestling with a lion: later he was said to have carried her to Libya where the city of Cyrene was named after her. Their son, Actaeon, was a mighty hunter of the type of Orion. He was devoured by his own hounds for boasting that he was a better hunter than Artemis. He also wanted to marry her and is therefore the male consort in a fertility rite, who ends up by being ritually torn to pieces. But when Artemis becomes the virgin huntress his fate is a punishment for seeing her naked.

Above. Death of Actaeon. Only some twenty years after the treatment by the Pan painter (*right*), that of the Lycaon painter shows an Increase in sensationalism which may owe something to drama. Artemis no longer acts, but stands by in a ritual pose with a torch while Zeus gives approval from the other side. But the hounds are maddened by Lyssa, Madness, who appears as a character in the *Heracles Mad* of Euripides, and Actaeon, with horns like Pan, tries to defend himself with his spears. The hounds may even have been figments of his imagination. Museum of Fine Arts, Boston, Massachusetts.

Above right. Death of Actaeon. The Pan painter, a master of the severe style of Attic vase painting about 460 B.C., was able to depict with intensity the terrifying heartlessness of the gods as they were conceived in the fifth century and in Greek tragedy. There is no trace of the original ritual. Artemis points her plague arrows at the offending Actaeon, who is merely identified by the hounds, since he is dying already. Museum of Fine Arts, Boston, Massachusetts. Pierce Fund.

Right. Death of Actaeon. Almost contemporary with the Pan painter's vase is a metope of the same scene from Temple E at Selinus. But the spirit of the work is quite different, because the very young Artemis looks on at the automatic consequence of her violated privacy with horrified compassion for her victim. The transformation of Actaeon into a stag is suggested by the horns which are indicated above him, and the dogs are naturistically treated. Museo Nazionale, Palermo.

Opposite. Cadmus and the serpent. The local potters working in Paestum in the fourth century produced some fine large vases with mythological subjects. Python, about 340 B.C., produced this copy of an earlier vase showing Cadmus killing the serpent which guarded the sacred spring on the site of Thebes. But he has added the huge pile of stones with one of which Cadmus, whose cap marks him as a foreigner, kills the snake. In his other hand he holds the water pot. The figure above the mirror is probably Harmonia, admiring the necklace she was given when she became Cadmus's bride. Hermes and Pan are introduced as spectators. Musée du Louvre, Paris.

Semele, Dionysus' mother, was loved by Zeus, who promised to grant her whatever she might ask, perhaps out of pleasure in her pregnancy. Semele asked him to appear to her in his divine form: she may have been put up to this by Hera, who appears as the jealous wife, or perhaps she was merely following an early practice by which the reigning pair imitated (or impersonated, or were held to be incarnations of) Zeus and Hera. Such mortal presumption shocked the later Greeks, and was always punished by the gods jealous of their prerogatives. So when Zeus, who could not escape from his promise, appeared to Semele she was consumed by the fire of his thunderbolt. Her tomb continued to smoulder: it may have contained a sacred flame marking the place where lightning had struck.

But Zeus snatched his unborn son from his mother's womb and sewed him into his own thigh, from where in due course he was born. Like the tale of the birth of Athena, this is a male myth expressing resentment and jealousy of woman's role in childbirth. Dionysus' name certainly contains the name of Zeus, and it may mean 'son of Zeus', just as Athena is 'daughter of aegis-bearing Zeus', or, possibly 'son-in-law'.

The newly born Dionysus was put out to nurse, first with Ino, his mother's sister, who dressed him in girl's clothes (a common custom to avert the evil eye, and practised on the Isle of Aran in Victorian times, but here said to be intended to hide the child from Hera), then with the nymphs of the legendary Mount Nysa, sometimes in the form of a kid. This story is very like that of the infancy of Zeus, on which it might conceivably have been based. But two strange stories in Pausanias suggest a ritual. The inhabitants of Prasiae on the eastern coast of the Peloponnese said that the dead Semele and the infant Dionysus were cast up by the sea in a chest, like that of Danae and the infant Perseus. They buried Semele, and Ino appeared in her wanderings to nurse Dionysus.

A similar chest, with an image of Dionysus in it, was given to a Thessalian, Eurypylus, as his share of the

Left. Dionysus on a goat. A popular type of terracotta statuette, especially in the fourth century and later, is a god or goddess in association with a possibly sacred animal. The connection of Dionysus with the goat may be ancient. He sometimes wears a goat skin himself and goats were sacrificed to him in some rituals. But his satyrs were always in Attica regarded as horses not as goats, and the explanation of tragedy as 'goat song' is not entirely satisfactory. Whatever the connection, however, it was enough for later artists, who developed the type of the youthful Dionysus to the point of effeminacy, a charge already brought against the god and his devotees by Euripides in the *Bacchae*. But the Greeks did not underestimate the power of a deity who became more and more associated with all ecstatic states, and not only those induced by the religious use of wine. British Museum, London.

Opposite. The infancy of Dionysus was important in myth, in which his nurses often feature. It is not common on vases until the fifth century, later in association with Hermes (though on one vase Zeus himself hands over his son), as in the illustration on page 52, where the child holds out his hands to a Maenad. In this white-figure version the child is given to a very sedate and reverend Father Silenus, far from the drunken old reprobate he is in Comedy and Satyr plays. The most famous representation of part of the scene is the Hermes of Praxiteles, found in the temple of Hera at Olympia: all of them owe much to the human concept of a young adult with his infant brother. Musei Vaticani.

spoils of Troy. The image drove him mad, and he made his way to Patrae, where he put an end to the annual sacrifice of a bridal pair to Artemis and became a hero at the annual festival of Dionysus. These stories suggest a regular ritual at which an infant Dionysus was brought to land in a chest, and then nursed.

It was in Phrygia that Dionysus discovered the vine, and taught men to make wine from it. From there he set out to convert the world, punishing those who refused to accept him. This pattern is a ritual one. The rout of women who went out into the hills was a normal part of the cult of Dionysus. They may have been taking out the old year and bringing in the new one, a type of ceremony well attested in Europe. But the stories may also reflect real opposition to a new and socially disruptive religion. The first such story is told in the *Iliad*. Lycurgus attacked the nurses of Dionysus, who fled into the sea where Thetis protected him. The gods punished Lycurgus with blindness and a short life.

Here the ritual role of the 'nurses' is clear: they are the Maenads who have found the new baby and brought him back. Dionysus flees into the sea because in other rituals it was from there that he came. As in the story of his infancy, there are reminiscences of the succession myth, with Thetis playing the grandmother role that she did for Zeus in the story of Briareus.

The *Iliad* has as usual suppressed the gorier details of the fate of Lycurgus. He went mad and attacked his son with an axe, thinking he was pruning a vine. The land became barren, and was made fruitful again when Lycurgus was torn to pieces by horses on Mount Pangaeus. Doubtless he was ritually eaten, and pieces of him strewn on the fields, though the horses seem to come from the ritual of the Thracian Ares, whose sons, like the Thracian Diomede, often own man-eating mares. The other elements clearly describe the Thracian vegetation cult. The son is also called Dryas, 'tree-man', and an Attic vase shows Dionysus worshipped in this form.

But the best known story is that told by Euripides of Dionysus' return to his birth-place, Thebes. Rejected there, Dionysus maddened the women and drove them to Mount Cithaeron, where they routed the troops sent against them. Pentheus imprisoned the effeminate male leader of the Bacchantes (who is clearly distinguished from Dionysus in the play), or he thought he did — in fact they caught a bull. The leader escaped, and persuaded Pentheus to put on women's dress and spy on the Bacchantes on the mountains. To do this he climbed a pine tree, which the Bacchantes uprooted and then tore him ritually to pieces, led by his mother Agave. She returned in triumph with the head of her son as a trophy, only to come to herself and learn the sad lesson of all Greek tragedies: mortal submission to the will of the stronger gods.

In Attica the worship of Dionysus was easily assimilated to a local cult, but the ritual death could not be avoided. Icarius gladly accepted the gift of the vine, and in the proper missionary spirit gave wine to some shepherds, who in ignorance drank it unmixed like water (the Greeks normally diluted it with at least three parts of water). In their madness, the shepherds, thinking they were poisoned, killed Icarius, whose daughter hanged herself when she found his body. This story explains the Athenian festival, paralleled in Italy, at which small images were set swinging in the branches of trees in the heat of summer, when Erigone, the daughter 'born in the spring', had been killed by the hot summer's drought.

Midas

In the course of his travels Dionysus encountered both Midas and Orpheus. Midas is a kind of King of Fairyland in popular Greek fables, the richest man in the world. His kingdom was finally settled as Phrygia, to where his fabulous rose-gardens were transferred from their original place in Macedonia. To these rose-gardens Silenus turned aside, the eldest of the satyrs, a fat old man with the snub nose and low forehead which was the Greek convention for such wild and lustful creatures. He fell asleep in Midas' garden, where a fountain had been filled with wine to catch him. Midas feasted him, and returned him to Dionysus, who granted him the boon he asked, that everything he touched might turn to gold.

But like a man who swears an oath, he was held to the literal meaning of his words, and when even the food he put to his lips turned to gold he was forced to ask that the gift be rescinded, a well known fairy tale motif. He was told to wash in the sands of the river Pactolus, all the sands of which turned to gold, thus fulfilling a prophecy made in his infancy, when ants carried grains of corn into his mouth while he was sleeping, showing that he would be the richest man on earth.

Orpheus

The mysteries of Orpheus were another ecstatic cult which spread in Greece in the hard times of the seventh century onwards. They resembled the cult of Dionysus, and Orpheus is always represented as one of his followers. His mythological chronology varies, but Aristaeus, husband of one of the daughters of Cadmus, appears in one of his stories. Orpheus was the son of Calliope, the muse of epic poetry (for his verses were in hexameters, like the *Iliad* and the *Odyssey* and the Boeotian poems of the school of Hesiod). He had a magic lyre, with which he charmed trees and rivers as well as the wild beasts: even stones gathered round him and danced, which sounds like another explanation of stone circles.

Orpheus loved a wood nymph, Eurydice, whom Aristaeus also loved and chased at her wedding. As she ran from him she trod upon a snake and was stung to death. Inconsolate, Orpheus followed her to Hades, and charmed Persephone into letting Eurydice go, on condition that he did not look behind him until he got her safely on the earth. Of course he failed to fulfil the condition and, rejecting all other women, he wandered with a band of Thracians preaching his own mysteries and those of Dionysus, until he was torn to pieces by Thracian Maenads, who were jealous for the honour of their sex. They cast his head into the river Hebrus, and it sang 'Eurydice, Eurydice' as it floated to the sea.

The story of Orpheus has attracted writers ever since Virgil, who ends his *Georgics* with the story and is the first surviving author to bring in the romantic motif of Aristaeus. He probably got this from the Alexandrian scholars but it might have a basis in a ritual sacrifice of a virgin. Eurydice's sisters took their revenge by making all Aristaeus' bees die: he learnt how to get a new swarm from the decaying carcass of a bullock, a superstition (for the bees are really a

Above. The capture of Silenus was a popular subject in Greek vase painting, but representations of the actual event are rare. This late-sixth-century vase by the Achelous painter is highly dramatic. The Silenus (not in any of the vases identified as the fat old Pappa Silenus but as a regular horse satyr) is taken by two hunters armed with two throwing spears in the very act of drinking at the fountain running with wine, which stands before a stylised olive tree. It is possible that a genre scene 'Hunters surprise a satyr' preceded its association with Midas and later moralisation, though an earlier vase shows a bound satyr brought before the king. Metropolitan Museum of Art, New York. Rogers Fund, 1949.

Left. Death of Orpheus. The work of the Achilles painter reflects the serene style of Periclean sculpture. It freezes into calm the action of a violent subject, the death of Orpheus. A severe Thracian woman, identified by the tattoos on her left forearm, prevents the dying Orpheus from destroying his lyre or striking her with it. Blood from a spear thrust runs down his right side. There is no hint of ritual tearing or of the head floating down the river. Museum of Fine Arts, Boston, Massachusetts. Special Fund.

Opposite. Hermes and the infant Dionysus. Hermes, recognised by his travelling cloak and hat, magic staff, and what look like formalised wings on his boots, holds the infant Dionysus, who reaches out towards a Maenad with a thyrsus. The nurses of Dionysus play a part in many ritual myths. In narrative mythology they were localised on Mount Nysa in Asia Minor, with which the name of the god was connected, and are described as nymphs. British Museum, London.

form of fly) shared by the ancient Hebrews. The prohibition on looking back is a folk-tale motif. Cronus in the succession myth and Deucalion after the flood both threw things over their shoulders without looking back. The singing head is a similar motif.

The Apotheosis of Dionysus

Dionysus too was said to have descended into Hades to bring up his mother Semele and conduct her to Olympus under her Greek name Thyone, the 'possessed'. Persephone or Koré, and in one version also Pandora, rise from the earth in this way, bringing back the spring, and Eurydice must be a deity of the same type. Dionysus descended through the bottomless Alcyonian lake in Argos by the spring of Lerna where annual mysteries were performed at night, the nature of which Pausanias refuses to divulge.

The arrival of Dionysus by sea may lie behind the myth told in the hexameter *Hymn* and illustrated on a famous vase. Dionysus was kidnapped by Etruscan pirates (in a later version he took passage with them for Naxos, where he had a cult involving Ariadne), who persisted in their intention even when they were unable to tie him up and despite the advice of the pious steersman. Out at sea suddenly the sail was wreathed in a fruiting vine and the mast and oars were twined in ivy. Ivy was much used in Bacchic rites, probably because it is evergreen and preserves the life of the vegetation spirit during the dead season.

The god became a lion on the foredeck, and made a she-bear appear amidships, driving the sailors to the stern where they huddled round the pious steersman. The lion seized their leader, and they all jumped into the sea and were turned into dolphins. But Dionysus stopped the steersman from following their example, revealed himself to him and made him rich. Presumably he too became a Dionysiac missionary.

The story is partly intended to explain the well-known friendliness of dolphins, who rescued the poet Arion in similar circumstances (an example of a myth being transferred to a historical personage). But chiefly it exhibits the manifest power of the god, who is shown by the painter Exekias as a huge bearded figure in a sailing ship like a dolphin, with two dolphins painted on its side fore and aft, and a bird-beaked stern. This is the early form in which the god is depicted, full of that quality which the Greeks never failed to attribute to their gods, whatever the stories they told of them, a quality that aroused in men feelings of reverent worship.

Left. Early fourth century 7-inch (18 cm) statuette found in a tomb at Locri in the hand of a female skeleton. If the tambourine originally belonged to it and is not the result of a mend in antiquity (since the figure seems to have three arms) it may identify a Maenad and have some religious significance from the Mysteries. But the pose is not wild, and it might be a doll or favourite ornament buried with a young and perhaps unmarried woman. Museo Nazionale, Reggio, Calabria.

Opposite. Earlier Athenian representations of Dionysus, such as this by the Amasis painter, who worked from 560 to 525 B.C., show him as a dignified and bearded elderly man (even sometimes as a tree with human head) rather than the effeminate youth of later representations. Here he receives the offering of a hare and a small deer from two fully clad and decorous maenads: only the ivy strands and the panther skin suggest the wilder elements of a cult which, it seems, had in Attica early been institutionalised (perhaps by Pisistratus), just as its earlier impersonation of animals and gods was formalised into Attic drama. Cabinet des Medailles, Bibliothèque Nationale, Paris.

55

The Children of Aeolus

Unlike Cadmus, Aeolus had sons as well as daughters. The stories about them seem to contain saga, that is, genuinely historical material however garbled and misplaced, as well as ritual elements. A large number of primitive motifs recur, and suggest a modified patriarchal system. Genealogies are normally reckoned in the male line, but sons rarely succeed fathers: they often marry their brother's daughter, as if that gave them a better title. They are more often sacrificed, sometimes by boiling in a cauldron, or they leave the country and marry another king's daughter, with whom, of course, they get the kingdom.

Conversely, kings often fear death at the hand of their daughter's son and take fruitless steps to avoid this fate. Sometimes they set up ritual contests for their daughter's hand, but their daughter betrays them to the right man. Sometimes they prevent their daughter's marriage, but she is impregnated by a god. Then they expose the child, but it is miraculously preserved to return as the promised supplanter. Their actions are often said to be motivated by an incestuous love of their own daughter, and at least one hero actually fathered a son in this way, at least keeping the succession in the male line. Their wives too join in the conspiracy against them, inviting young men who visit their husbands to kill their host and take over his wife and the kingdom. Then sons avenge their father's death by killing their mother.

This bald catalogue of incest, adultery, parricide and matricide provides the raw material for most Greek tragedies, which took their plots from heroic mythology. The tragedians' concentration on such themes reflects the tensions of Athenian social and family life. But the original stories are not to be explained only in terms of individual psychology or of essential human wickedness. In many cases they are simply the consequence of the strong interaction of two completely incompatible social structures.

The important children of Aeolus are four sons and three daughters: the rest seem to be genealogical fictions. The four sons are Athamas, Sisyphus, Salmoneus and Cretheus, and the three daughters Alcyone, Canace, and Calyce.

Athamas

Athamas, king of Orchomenus, a Mycenaean site on the Thessalian side of Boeotia, seems to have practised rain magic like his ancestor Deucalion. Athamas married Nephele, whose name means 'cloud': she may have been a fairy like the Swanmaiden, whom Athamas captured by stealing her clothes, although such stories are told in Greek only of sea nymphs like Thetis. At any rate she is evidence for her husband's concern with rain-making. In a drought he proposed to sacrifice his son Phrixus on Mount Laphystius but Zeus sent a golden ram on which Phrixus made his escape with his sister Helle. He reached Colchis at the far end of the Black Sea, where Aeetes was king. Helle fell off on the way and the Hellespont is named after her. But Phrixus sacrificed the ram to Zeus of Escapes, to whom also Deucalion had sacrificed after the flood, and hung up its fleece in a sacred grove.

Later in Thessaly, Athamas was about to suffer the same fate of sacrifice to Zeus Laphystius when his grandson, who had returned from Colchis, rescued him. In consequence, the eldest male of the line of Athamas and Phrixus had for some time been liable to sacrifice if he entered the council chamber there, an act by which he was presumably deemed to have become king. It is doubtful, however, if the sacrifice was ever more than simulated in the time of Herodotus, who reports the custom.

This sacrifice does not seem to be part of the rain magic. Athamas was liable to be sacrificed at the end of his term, or when he lost his virility, or in emergency, like any sacred king in the *Golden Bough*. He was sacrificing his son as his surrogate or substitute. The golden ram seems to have been an emblem of sovereignty, with which Phrixus was temporarily invested, and not 'a ram caught in a thicket'. It was the animal form of the god.

Later the sacrifice of Phrixus was accounted for by the wiles of a wicked step-mother. Athamas took as his second wife Ino the daughter of Cadmus. By her he had two children, in whose interests their mother wanted to be rid of Phrixus and Helle. So she parched the seedcorn and persuaded the oracle (always the sign of a later version) to require their sacrifice to cure the famine.

For their part in rearing Dionysus, Athamas and Ino were driven mad and killed their children: Melicertes was boiled in a cauldron and then Ino jumped into the sea with him. They were worshipped, especially at Corinth, as Leucothea, the White Goddess, and the infant Palaemon, and are in fact a mother-goddess and consort, the former identified with the nurse of Dionysus, perhaps because the child came from the sea. Athamas killed the other child and went into exile in Thessaly.

Salmoneus also seems to have practised rain-magic, imitating Zeus by dragging cauldrons behind his chariot for thunder and throwing out torches for lightning. So too his sister Alcyone and her husband Ceyx called each other Hera and Zeus. This identification — rather than impersonation — was required of early kings. But the later Greeks considered it blasphemous. Salmoneus was blasted by real lightning, and Alcyone and Ceyx

were turned into the sea birds whose names they bear. The halcyon was said to nest on the sea in the winter, and during these 'halcyon days' the sea remained calm. The lake by which Dionysus entered Hades was called Alcyonian, and the story may therefore have reminiscences of the chest that brought the child to land.

Pelias

Sisyphus is said, in an obscure story, to have hated Salmoneus, and to have been told that if he had children by Salmoneus' daughter Tyro they would avenge him. In fact, Tyro appears as married to the other brother, Cretheus. She bore twins to a god, Poseidon, who assumed the form of the river Enipeus, for which she conceived a passion. One of the sons, Pelias, avenged her on Cretheus' second wife, who mistreated her (perhaps the second wife in such cases was married under the patriarchal rules) and probably on Cretheus as well, since Pelias inherited the kingdom. He is, of course, represented as a villainous usurper, who killed Sidero on the altars of Hera. He was in turn supplanted, and indeed sacrificed by boiling in a cauldron, by Cretheus' grandson, Jason.

Pelias and his brother were exposed in a chest, but saved by the herdsman in charge of a troop of brood mares when one of them drew his attention to the children by kicking Pelias in the face. Poseidon often appears in the form of a stallion, just as Demeter, his original consort, appears in that of a mare: so it is possible that Pelias was the divine twin and marked as such by his father. When they were fully grown they returned to Iolcus, the city of Cretheus, where they were recognised by the tokens of identity which they had worn when they were exposed. It was then that Pelias avenged his mother. But he quarrelled with his mortal brother Neleus who went off to Pylos.

There has obviously been some substitution and suppression in this part of the story of the sons of Aeolus and their families, but it none the less exhibits many features of the pattern of interacting forms of succession.

Phrixus and the Golden Ram. The artistic type of the god or goddess riding upon an animal is one that may go back to a period when god and animal were even more closely identified. It recurs in a number of myths of heroes, such as Europa and the bull and, as here, Phrixus on the Golden Ram, and even perhaps Odysseus escaping from the Cyclops' cave. This late version in terracotta, perhaps towards 435 B.C., shows Phrixus not riding but holding on to a ram that appears to be swimming the Hellespoint. It may have been balanced on the large wooden chest for which it was designed (it is 10 inches [25.5 cm] long) by a figure of Helle on the ram, for an earlier figure of her, shown seated on the ram like Europa on her bull, faces left.
Metropolitan Museum of Art, New York, Rogers Fund, 1912.

Apart from the one obscure story, the role of Sisyphus has been completely lost, and all the other myths about him contain fairy-tale motifs.

Sisyphus

Sisyphus, with the keenest eye for profit of any man, lived at Corinth where his tomb was, 'though even of the Corinthians of his own time there were few who knew where it was'. The sons of Aeolus were widely dispersed in Greece: Salmoneus went to Elis, and it is likely that the quarrel he or Cretheus had with Sisyphus was about the inheritance. Such quarrels, especially between twin brothers, are another recurrent motif in the stories, and they too are probably a consequence of the social structure.

Because of his reputation, Sisyphus is brought into association with two other heroes of similar character, Autolycus, 'who surpassed other men in thieving and the oath', and Odysseus, whose real father was sometimes said

Opposite. Delphi. The reconstructed columns of the fourth-century temple are seen from above, looking south-east up the valley to the pass.

Below. The identification of un-named subjects in ancient art is often uncertain. This Laconian cup, from Sparta, may represent two Titans, Atlas holding up the heavens and Prometheus punished by the eagle eating his liver. The snake, however, is common in Laconian pictures of the heroised dead, and may indicate that the scene is in the underworld, in which case it is Sisyphus holding, rather than rolling, the stone, and the figure devoured by the eagle must be Tityus, whose punishment for attempting to rape Leto is so described in the *Odyssey*. The author is inclined to favour the first alternative. Musei Vaticani.

to be Sisyphus and whose mother was
Autolycus' daughter. One of Autolycus' thefts was that of a boar's tusk
helmet, which he took from Eleon son
of Amyntor Ormenides. Such helmets
are known from the shaft graves excavated by Schliemann at Mycenae:
so perhaps Autolycus was a tomb-
robber. But Sisyphus outwitted him.
When Autolycus stole his cattle and
changed their colour, Sisyphus
marked their hooves, and so recognised his own and got them back.
This looks like a rationalised version
of the exploit of Hermes, Autolycus'
father, and of the invention of brand-
ing (the Corinthians used Q, the original form of the first letter of their
town).

Finally Sisyphus cheated Death and
took him prisoner, so that nobody
died until Ares released him. Then
Sisyphus told his wife to leave his
body unburied, and persuaded Hades
to let him return to repair this impious omission, probably swearing
some crafty oath which made Hades
think he would return at once, instead
of on some future occasion. Details

are not preserved of this folk-tale, a
kind of story generally alien to the
temper of Greek mythology. But he
is one of the great sinners whom
Odysseus saw punished in Hades,
pushing up a hill a stone which con-
tinually rolled back to the bottom.
This punishment suggests the Titans
under their mountains.

Endymion
The other two daughters of Aeolus
belong rather to religion. Canace bore
four sons to Poseidon, one of whom,
Aloeus, married his brother's daughter Iphimedia. But her children were
sons of Poseidon, Otus and Ephialtes

who piled Pelion on Ossa. Calyce was
the mother of Endymion, another of
the Handsome Hunters carried off by
a goddess. The Moon took him to
Asia and bore him fifty daughters. He
sleeps for ever eternally young in a
cave on Mount Latmus in Caria. Presumably, like all such sleepers, he will
awake one day. But his tomb was also
shown in the stadium at Olympia in
Elis, and he is said to have made his
sons hold chariot races for the inheritance. There is also a story that he
was admitted to Olympus, but expelled and cast asleep for an attempt
on Hera: this is appropriate behaviour for a mighty hunter.

The Monster-Killers

There is no lack of monsters in very early Greece, whether in Minoan and Mycenaean art or in mythology, in which Typhon, the opponent of Zeus in the succession myth, is the great-grandfather of all monsters. This and other conflicts with monsters have all sometimes been derived from religious ritual of the Near East, where the artistic type of hero and monster is very early. Certainly the great period for monsters in Greek art in the seventh century, when Gorgons (with or without Perseus), Sphinxes, Sirens and, but less commonly, Chimaeras abound in the 'orientalising' art of the time. But the myths are earlier than this: the two great mortal monster-killers, Bellerophon and Perseus, are already known in Homeric and Hesiodic poetry. They involve both Aeolids and Danaids, though the genealogies will not synchronise.

Perseus was a descendant of Danaus by Acrisius, one of the twin grandsons of Hypermnestra, the virtuous Danaid who did not kill her husband. The twins, Acrisius and Proetus, strove even in the womb. But there is no story of their begetting, which might be expected to have been the work of a god: perhaps the story was suppressed in the interests of a genealogy in the male line. Later, when fully grown, they fought for the kingdom. The result was a draw, and the two brothers were reconciled. This was probably a trick, as in other similar stories; for Acrisius then drove out Proetus, who went to Lycia and married the king's daughter. But his father-in-law Iobates restored Proetus to Tiryns, while Acrisius continued to rule at Argos.

The only unusual element in this story, which follows a regular pattern, is that it mentions Lycia. There were a number of epic traditions about Lycia. The Lycians play a large, but geographically unlikely, part in the fighting of the *Iliad,* much of it against the Myrmidons under Patroclus. This might reflect Mycenaean settlement there (so far unattested) rather than the later Greek migrations to Asia Minor.

Bellerophon

Bellerophon was the grandson of Sisyphus. He left Corinth, exiled for the murder of his brother, and came to Proetus at Tiryns. He was later recognised as 'being the noble offspring of a god', Poseidon, who in his horse form was also the father of the winged horse Pegasus by Medusa, the mortal Gorgon.

Bellerophon was remarkable for his beauty. The wife of Proetus, Antia in Homer, later Sthenoboea, asked him to lie with her and, when he refused, accused him before Proetus, saying 'May you die, O Proetus, or kill Bellerophon'. This is the motif of the virtuous Joseph: but the wife is not originally wanton, merely playing her part in a regular succession pattern. Bellerophon's refusal is a deliberate rejection of that pattern, but in an earlier version he may have killed his host, as Gyges did King Candaules of Lydia in Herodotus.

As it was, Proetus was convinced, though the rules of hospitality prevented him from killing Bellerophon himself. Instead 'he sent him to Lycia, and gave him baleful signs, having graved on a folded tablet many spirit-destroying things', orders for his own death which he was to show to the king of Lycia. The 'baleful signs' are certainly a reference to writing, the power of which impressed an illiterate people first encountering it, but they are hardly, as has been suggested, the sole surviving recollection of the Mycenaean Linear B.

Iobates made a number of fruitless attempts to arrange Bellerophon's death. First he sent him against the Chimaera, a monstrous goat with the head of a lion and the tail of a snake. Bellerophon killed her from the back of Pegasus, the gift of his father Poseidon, on which indeed he may have come from Greece. For Pegasus is firmly located at Corinth, where Bellerophon caught him and Athena bridled him: the winged horse is the badge of the coins of Corinth.

Then Bellerophon was sent on two expeditions, one against the Solymians and one against the Amazons. On the way back from the latter he was ambushed by a picked band of Lycians: none of them returned home, for Bellerophon slew the lot. After this genuine saga of Lycian war, which has been assimilated to the pattern of exploits by which the king's supplanter is selected, Bellerophon married the king's daughter and became king of Lycia. But he came to a bad end: first he returned to Greece and carried off Sthenoboea, whom he cast into the sea from the back of

Pegasus; then he tried to ride up to heaven, an impiety for which he was thrown off Pegasus and lamed when he fell to earth. After that he wandered about as an outcast, although to go to heaven and dine with the gods was originally the prerogative of a divine king.

Bellerophon's daughter lay with Zeus and bore Sarpedon, for whose death at Troy Zeus 'poured bloody drops of rain to the earth honouring his dear son, whom Patroclus was going to kill'. The twin brothers, Sleep and Death, carried his body to Lycia for embalming and burial. But

Above left and right. Stater from Corinth, 325–308 B.C. The winged horse Pegasus, on the obverse, though born from the Gorgon's blood in the African desert, was always at home in Corinth, where Bellerophon, himself originally a Corinthian, caught it and bridled it with the help of Athena. The Corinthians put Pegasus and Athena on their coinage, only bringing the type up to date from time to time. Athena's helmet, on the reverse, worn back to show the face and not down as in war, has the leather neckpiece showing under it. The boar and the letter P (the Greek R) are mint marks dating the issue. The Q under Pegasus stands for Corinth. Private collection.

Right. A very fierce and convincing Chimaera appears on an amphora by the Swing painter in the second half of the sixth century. It is nearly as tall as a man, and a wild goat rears out of its back, so that it can attack two men at once. There is, however, no trace of the snake on its tail. The type of Bellerophon and the Chimaera was well established by this time, and though Chimaeras appear alone, there is no other picture of a Chimaera hunt like this. The figure on the right with a club has been identified as Heracles, and the other on the left, with some kind of bent weapon, hardly a sword, as his companion Iolaus. There is indeed a nude Heracles without attributes on the other side of the vase but no surviving legend associates Heracles with the Chimaera. British Museum, London.

Opposite. A 'Melian relief' of Bellerophon and the Chimaera. It was made in the middle of the fifth century B.C. either as decoration for a chest or for suspension on the wall as a decoration. It has been restored from other examples of the same type. Bellerophon's body and the horse's front legs were missing, but the restorations can be regarded as certain. Bellerophon's posture, which suggests Mithras killing the bull, is made necessary by the goat's head which has turned an ordinary lioness into the monster, with the addition of a snake's head at the end of her tail. British Museum, London.

Sarpedon's mother died at the hands of Artemis, probably a piece of ritual survival, just as it seems likely that Bellerophon originally died at the hands of his supplanter Sarpedon.

Perseus

This was the fate also of Acrisius at the hands of Perseus, the 'Destroyer', perhaps like other names really a nickname intended to conceal the real name, knowledge of which gave power over its owner. In a vain effort to avoid his fate, Acrisius shut his daughter Danae up in an underground chamber made of bronze, a recurring motif. But Zeus impregnated her in the form of a shower of gold pouring into her lap, the primitive theory also found in the stories of Iphimedia and Tyro. The gold suggests that the underground chamber might be a tomb as rich in grave goods as the Mycenaean shaft graves.

As happens in the ritual of so many divine children, Perseus and his mother were cast adrift on the sea in a chest. It drifted to the island of Seriphus, where it was picked up in fishing nets. The king of Seriphus wanted to marry Danae, and so got rid of Perseus, sending him to get the Gorgon's head. Perseus behaved like a poor boy in a folktale, and made the rash promise when he was asked to provide a present. Of course he succeeded, and on his return killed the king just in time to prevent the marriage. So he behaves as a supplanter in two places: but in Seriphus the myth has had to be altered to take account of Perseus' Argive genealogy.

Left. Danae and the Shower of Gold. In the fifth century some Attic vase painters illustrated the more human aspects of the legend of Perseus, perhaps reflecting Attic drama. Danae is preparing for bed, untying one of the scarves that hold her hair, when she is surprised by the descent of the gold. The pose suggests that earth fertilised by the rain. Hermitage Museum, Leningrad.

Below left. Obverse of four drachma piece from Athens 530–520 B.C. When the Athenians began their commercial expansion about 520 B.C., they introduced the famous coinage with the head of Athena and the owl that was known all over the Greek world as 'Attic owls'. The earlier and purely local coinage used other symbols, such as this gorgon's head, which existed as a charm long before it was attached to the Gorgon. In this case it probably suggests the aegis of Athena. Cabinet des Medailles, Musée du Louvre, Paris.

Opposite. Perseus slaying the Gorgon. The second sixth-century temple at Selinus (temple C) still survives and the metopes have been excavated in fragments from it. They are in a far heavier style than those of the earlier temple, one of which showed Europa and the Bull (page 47), and all the characters are shown full face. It is for this reason and not to avoid being turned to stone, that Perseus is not looking at the Gorgon, whose head is in the form of the old gorgon mask. He kills her with a simple sword, but is shown with the winged boots of Hermes. The goddess behind him, who may have worn the aegis, is Athena. Medusa holds an unwinged Pegasus, her child by Poseidon who presumably visited her in the form of a stallion. Museo Nazionale, Palermo.

The Gorgon's head seems to have had an independent existence as a magical symbol to ward off evil long before it was attached to Medusa. But for Perseus the Gorgon Medusa was a monster to be slain. She had a horrible head with two tusks and a protruding tongue, and snakes for hair. Yet Poseidon had loved her, and she bore him two children, the winged horse Pegasus and the giant Chrysaor. This and her name, which means 'ruler', suggest that she was once the earth-mother in the form of a horse from a version of the succession myth in which Poseidon was the chief god.

Perseus killed the Gorgon in fairytale manner with the help of marvellous magic gifts from the gods or from some nymphs. They comprised winged sandals from Hermes; the cap of Hades, which made him invisible; a wallet called *cibisis* into which he put the head but which may originally have been a neverfailing magic source of supplies for the journey; a polished shield, in which to see the Gorgon without being turned to stone; and a special weapon, the *harpe*, half sword, half sickle, which possibly suggests the original succession myth.

Thus equipped, he made his way to the Gorgon and her sisters who were usually located in the African desert. There they were guarded by the three

aged sisters, who shared a single eye. Perseus stole the eye, and thus either evaded the sisters or blackmailed them into letting him pass and showing him the way. Thus he was enabled to come upon the Gorgon asleep.

Various legends are attached to the death of the Gorgon. Many of them concern Athena, who wore the Gorgon's head on her goatskin aegis (an early form of shield: the Gorgon's head is a favourite device on hoplite shields) as befits a war goddess. Medusa's children were said to have sprung from her dying body, probably from her spilt blood, as the Furies were from that of Uranus. Chrysaor, named after the golden sword his father left as token of paternity, himself fathered the three-bodied giant Geryon whom Heracles killed.

Athena invented the pipes to imitate the dying hiss of the snakes in the Gorgon's hair. But when she saw how her cheeks were distended in playing them, she cast them away. The abandoned pipes were picked up by a satyr, Marsyas, who challenged Apollo to a musical duel, pipes against lyre, and was winning until Apollo reversed the lyre and continued playing, a trick which Marsyas could not do with the pipes. Whereupon Apollo flayed Marsyas alive, cutting off all his skin with a knife, a fate which might reflect some primitive and barbaric Asian sacrifical ritual. Midas was the judge of a similar musical contest between Pan and Apollo, and for deciding against Apollo was punished with ass's ears, which he tried to conceal under his Phrygian cap. He

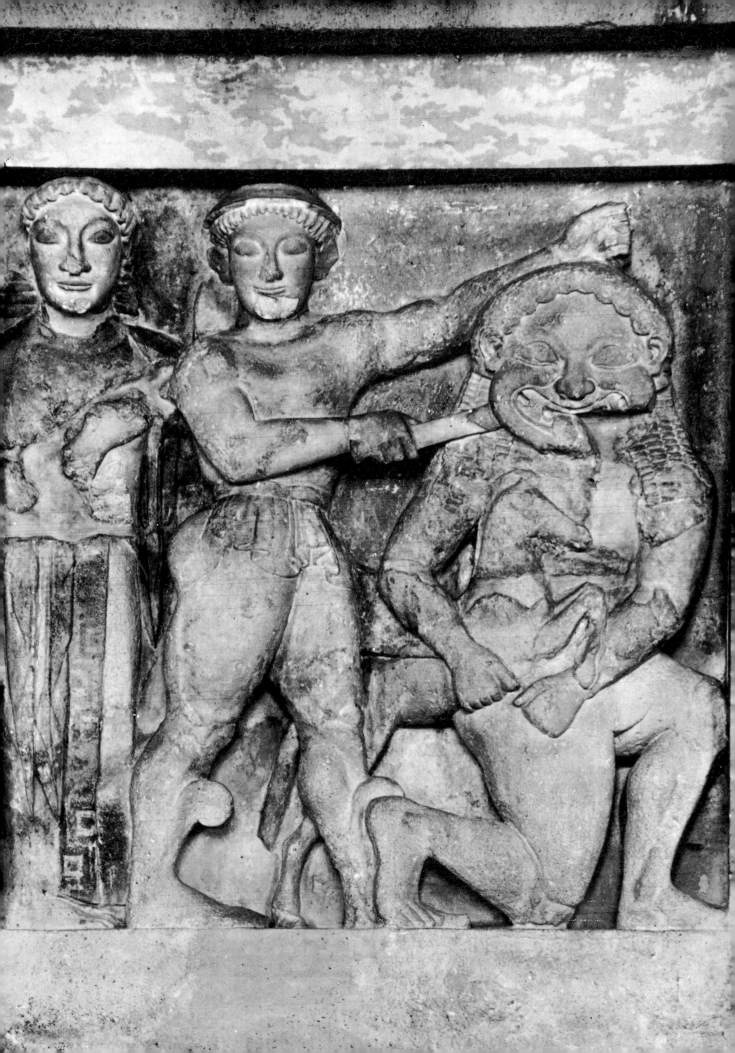

revealed their existence only to his barber, who tried to relieve himself of the intolerable burden of the secret by digging a hole in the earth in a secluded spot, into which he whispered the secret. But the reeds which grew up from the hole broadcast the secret.

Returning from killing the Gorgon, Perseus was involved in yet another supplanter story to get himself a bride. Cassiopeia, wife of Cepheus, king of Joppa, now Jaffa, boasted that she was fairer than the daughters of Nereus, which probably means that she impersonated or was identified with a sea goddess. Poseidon punished this blasphemy by sending a sea monster, from which Perseus delivered the king's daughter, Andromeda, by turning it to stone with the Gorgon's head (a story probably told to explain an off-shore rock). He also had to save her from her father's brother, who wanted to marry her.

Then Perseus returned to Seriphus and turned Polydectes and his court into a stone circle. His action is variously justified: either he saved his mother whom the king was trying to starve to death at the altar where she had taken refuge (it was no sacrilege to deny a suppliant food) or he was asked to bring his contribution to a banquet and teased into taking out the Gorgon's head. When Perseus returned with his mother and bride to Argos, Acrisius fled to Larissa in Thessaly, where Perseus visited him, only to cause his death by an unlucky cast of the discus. This death suggests a form of contest, to decide the supplanter, which was 'fixed' in order that the blood guilt might fall upon an inanimate object.

Opposite. Perseus and the Gorgon. Not only wood but also ivory has been preserved from the shrine of Hera at Samos. Ivory is a very easy material to work, and objects made in it often appear less primitive than other objects of the same date. This early-sixth-century relief shows strong oriental influence, just as the myth of Perseus and the Gorgon fits easily into the context of oriental myths of gods and monsters. The gorgon mask is, however, of the conventional type: the Gorgon herself was shown as a winged maiden and the hero under the direct protection of the goddess, here Athena, though her attributes have not survived. National Archaeological Museum, Athens.

Above. This late archaic vase by the Eucharides painter, of the early fifth century, (he takes his name from that of a 'beautiful boy' whose name is on one of his pots), more probably shows Acrisius overseeing the despatch of Danae and Perseus in the chest than its arrival at Seriphus. Though slapdash in style, the picture is dramatic in content, and the columns might suggest its derivation from a play. Museo Nazionale Archeologico, Ferrara.

The Great Exploits

Bellerophon and Perseus performed individual exploits and became the founders of ruling dynasties, in Lycia and in Mycenae. For Perseus did not take up the inheritance of Acrisius in Argos, but exchanged kingdoms with Megapenthes, the heir of Proetus at Tiryns. From there he is said to have founded Mycenae. Various stories were told to account for the name, the ending of which is pre-Greek. Either the cap fell off his scabbard, or he picked a mushroom, thus discovering a spring. The Greek for both objects is *myces*. The exchange of kingdoms suggests the dual kingship and picks up the rivalry of Acrisius and Proetus.

Communal Exploits

The exploits of the generations after Bellerophon and Perseus are more frequently co-operative. A number of the heroes of one generation, in addition to their personal mythology, are brought together for some great communal enterprise which seems, in most cases, to have formed the material of an epic poem. The *Iliad*, describing essentially, though in its own highly sophisticated literary way, the history of the Trojan war, is the only one of these epics which has survived.

The four great communal exploits of Greek mythology, the Calydonian Boar Hunt, the Argonautic expedition to the Black Sea, the Seven against Thebes and the Siege of Troy, are all related to places of importance in the Mycenaean period and (some of them) less so in later Greece. This, with other evidence, led the Swedish scholar Nilsson to postulate the Minoan-Mycenaean origin of Greek mythology. It is tempting to find in them evidence for some form of Mycenaean confederacy, under the he-gemony of Mycenae, which has more tombs, and especially more tholos tombs, than are linked to any other single site, and which is linked by surviving Mycenaean roads and bridges with other Mycenaean sites in the Argolid. However, it must be stressed that we know almost nothing of the relation between Mycenaean cities (only something of the internal workings of a 'palace economy' at Pylos, a comparatively small area) and it must remain debatable whether these exploits are any more than poetic invention of a later period.

The *Iliad* also refers to Meleager, chief hero of the Calydonian Boar hunt, and makes one reference to the funeral games of Oedipus, which belong to a Theban cycle which ended in the failure of the Seven against Thebes and the success of their sons, the Epigoni, 'those born after'.

The *Odyssey* was conceived as a later sequel to the *Iliad*, and succeeds in dealing incidentally with the fates of almost all the heroes who fought at Troy in the course of narrating that of Odysseus. But the story of his wanderings, though very largely made up of motifs from fairy and folk tales, seems also to have drawn on the last of these lost epics, which told the tale of the *Argo* and Jason's quest for the Golden Fleece.

These communal enterprises may be partly a literary device to group the stories of a number of heroes around a central theme. But they may also reflect something of the political organisation of Greece under the Mycenaeans, who built their cities at points of strategic importance, linked them with at least the rudiments of a communications system, and fortified them not only, perhaps, against each other but also against a subject

Below. Delphi perhaps owed its reputation as a sacred shrine to the landscape. A stream and a spring descend in a cleft between the Phaedriades Rocks, with Parnassus rising behind them. The cleft joins a narrow but remarkably fertile valley which leads east up to the pass where the roads divide and Oedipus killed his father, and south-west down to the sea. The sacred site looks south. The precinct was walled in the middle of the sixth century B.C., when a large polygonal wall was built, partly destroying the earlier sanctuary of Gaia, the earth, in order to support a large archaic temple. On this site and to the same plan a fourth-century temple was built in 320 B.C. after the earlier one had collapsed in 373. The six reconstructed columns of this last temple are shown, looking south to the hills across the valley which hides the sea.

population. For all these sagas are connected with Mycenaean cities, Thebes, Orchomenus and the port Iolcus, Argos and Mycenae (together with Troy which is culturally related).

The Theban stories stand apart from the rest, though Argives took part in the attacks on Thebes. One consequence of the sack of Thebes was that Thebans play little part in the siege of Troy. The Trojan war is the culminating episode of Greek mythology. But the exploits of the Calydonian Boar hunt and the Voyage of the Argonauts are fitted on to the heroic genealogies especially of the children of Aeolus.

The Calydonian Boar Hunt

The dynasty at Calydon in Aetolia claimed descent from Aeolus by Endymion. It has its share of the sons of gods: Evenus was son of Ares, and therefore the owner of (probably maneating) mares with which he ran chariot races against the suitors of his daughter Marpessa. When they lost he nailed their skulls to his house walls. He was defeated by the divine one of a pair of Spartan twins, Idas,

brother of Lynceus. Idas was son of Poseidon, who gave him a winged chariot with which he beat Evenus, and carried off his daughter. The race, or the pursuit, ended at a river, which Idas could presumably cross in his winged chariot. In disgust Evenus killed his horses and threw himself and them into the river which was given his name.

This variant of the myth of the supplanter is clearly based on a local ritual of chariot race and sacrifice, which recurs in the story of Pelops and lies behind some of the Olympic games. But the story of Idas is further complicated, because he then fell in with Apollo, and fought him for the hand of Marpessa. Zeus separated them and allowed Marpessa to choose the one she wanted. She chose Idas, for she feared that Apollo would desert her in her old age. In one version Apollo begot a son on Marpessa to supplant Evenus.

The cousin of Evenus in the male line was Oeneus, 'wine man', said to have been the first to receive the vine from Dionysus. He got it, and his nickname, by abandoning his wife for

The Calydonian Boar hunt. This is the other side of the band cup signed by two potters or potter and painter, Archicles and Glaucytes, which is shown in black and white on page 108. Two of the most popular exploits in archaic art, about 540 B.C., are shown on the vase: Theseus and the Minotaur on the other side and the Calydonian Boar hunt on the side shown. All the characters and their dogs are labelled, but there is no sign of Atalanta as there is on the earlier François vase which in many ways may have been its model. To the right are Meleager with his bitch Thero, Peleus (who killed his host Eurytion by mistake), Melanion and Cimon with a dog Podargos (swift-foot). On the other side are Castor and Pollux, Mopsus the seer, and Jason and Idasus (perhaps = Idas) with the dogs Gorgus and Charon. The names show that the literary tradition of the hunt as a communal exploit was well known. The white dog on top of the boat, which is as tall as a man, is appropriately called Leucius, 'Whitey'. The mangled remains of Podes lie below. Staatliche Antikensammlungen und Glyptothek, Munich.

Atalanta. The earliest mosaic pavements are found in Greece from 400 B.C. made from natural pebbles. But the developed art is Hellenistic and it became extremely popular among the Romans. In the fourth century A.D. hunting scenes were especially liked, and Atalanta was portrayed as the type of the huntress. Her quarry in this mosaic was not the Calydonian Boar but a lion, now lost, and she was balanced by Meleager hunting a leopard. At the other end of a large room in a villa at Halicarnassus was a mosaic of the hunt of Dido and Aeneas. This combination of Greek and Roman mythological motifs, and of eroticism and hunting is notable. British Museum, London.

Dionysus so as to beget a daughter, a version which suggests he started as a primitive wine-god. But the daughter Deianeira drove a chariot as a war-maiden, and so her father may in some versions have been Ares, who was also said to have been the father of Oeneus' son Meleager. Meleager led the heroes in the Calydonian Boar hunt, as a result of which he himself met his fate.

Artemis was angry with Oeneus because he had failed to sacrifice to her the first-fruits of his vine-yard. This is the motif of the neglected fairy: for he had sacrificed to the other gods. But some vine-yard ritual may lie behind the story. She sent a huge boar which ravaged the land, especially, no doubt, the vines. The combined heroes succeeded in killing

this monster, though at some cost to themselves, but a quarrel arose over the spoils. Artemis saw to it that the whole enterprise (like all the rest of these great exploits) brought no good to any of those engaged in it.

The quarrel in fact arose over Atalanta, a virgin huntress who is obviously a form of Artemis and as such needed for the Boar hunt. In her story, elements from the myths of Artemis and her nymphs are mixed with others taken from those of the sons of gods. Thus she was exposed by her father, who wanted a son, but was suckled by a bear, Artemis' animal. She made her suitors run a foot race for her hand, and put them to death if they lost, but was punished for the eventual loss of her virginity by being turned into a lion. Like Callisto, she

is said to have violated a sanctuary of Zeus, perhaps that on Mount Lycaeus. Those who entered it lost their shadows and were hunted to death or exile as 'stags' like Actaeon. One of the two alternative genealogies of Atalanta made her Arcadian, the other a Boeotian descendant of Aeolus.

The famous golden apples with which Melanion prevented Atalanta from overtaking him are a fairy tale motif, like the magic objects thrown out in the 'flight from the enchanter' to become impenetrable thickets and mountains. They have become apples, and the gift of Aphrodite, because an apple was the traditional love gift of the Greeks. They have really nothing to do with the Hesperides. Despite her marriage, Atalanta's son was called Parthenopaeus, 'unmarried woman's child', and the father was sometimes said to be Ares or Meleager.

The quarrel over the spoils of the Calydonian Boar was caused by Meleager's love for Atalanta. Atalanta was the first to hit the boar, but Meleager killed it. So he was awarded the skin, which he gave to Atalanta. His mother's brothers (who are always important in societies organised on matrilinear principles) objected, and claimed it by family right. In the ensuing war Meleager killed them, and his mother cursed him, so that he withdrew from the fighting and locked himself into his chamber with his wife. He refused to come out, despite the pleas of his father and mother, until the city was about to be sacked, when he yielded to the pleas of his wife and delivered the city, presumably at the cost of his own life.

For his mother did more than merely curse him. She prayed for the death of her son, a prayer which the Fury heard. She actually caused his death by putting back on to the fire the brand in which the 'external soul' of Meleager was lodged, and which she had taken from the fire when he was seven days old. Meleager was in fact put to death for refusing to accept the claims of matrilinear descent, though his story, as told in the *Iliad*, contains elements which seem

to derive from the sacrifice of a son, probably as a surrogate for his father, to save the city in a grave emergency.

Many of the heroes who were present at the Calydonian Boar hunt also appear as Argonauts. Jason, their leader, is the grandson of Cretheus in the male line, and the Quest for the Golden Fleece is the test by which the supplanter is selected. Like Perseus, Jason is tricked into going for it: Pelias asked him how he would destroy an enemy, and Jason answered, 'by sending him for the Fleece'.

Melampus
Melampus, Jason's cousin, learnt the language of birds and animals: for when an oak was felled, he saved the young snakes that lived in it, and in gratitude they cleaned out his ears with their tongues. He used this knowledge to get his brother Bias a bride, the daughter of Neleus. The bride-price was the cattle of Phylacus, which were guarded by a wonderful hound which nothing could escape. Melampus let himself be caught and put into prison. There he heard the worms saying that they would gnaw through the beam the next night, and established his reputation by asking for a new cell. Impressed, Phylacus asked how to cure the impotence of his son, which had been magically caused when he put a gelding knife in a sacred oak, as a bird told Melampus. The rust of that knife cured the wound it had caused. As his reward, Melampus got the oxen, and his brother his bride.

Admetus
Admetus was another cousin of Jason. Apollo served him as cowherd, and made all his cows drop twins. This special relationship was explained as Apollo's penance for killing the Cyclops who made the thunderbolt with which Zeus killed Asclepius for raising the dead. This deed had offended Hades and made men immortal like gods. Asclepius was Apollo's son by a mortal woman, Coronis, who later played him false with another mortal. This story, like that of Marpessa, may reflect the theory that one twin had a divine

father and the other a mortal one. But Apollo killed Coronis, and either he or Hermes snatched the child from her womb on the pyre.

This legend assimilates the birth of Asclepius to that of Dionysus. But the Epidaurians, who had a cult of Asclepius involving 'incubation', sleeping in the temple to learn the cure by a dream, told a typical story of exposure, on a mountain called Nipple, and feeding by goats. Various men were listed as having been raised from the dead by Asclepius. Some of them may have been originally 'dying gods' whose stories included resurrection, like Lycurgus the surrogate of Dionysus.

Apollo won for Admetus his bride, Alcestis, daughter of Pelias, by performing for him the required exploit of yoking a lion and a boar to a chariot. But Admetus was doomed to an early death, and found the marriage chamber full of snakes sent by Artemis. Apollo made the Fates drunk, and extracted from them the concession that Admetus might live if any could be found to die for him. Only his wife would do so: but Persephone sent her up to earth again. Euripides introduces Heracles to wrestle with Death for the life of Alcestis, but in the original story can be seen the sacred king, with whom is bound up the fertility of the realm, and whose wife impersonates the Girl and returns from the underworld in the spring.

Jason and the Argonauts
Admetus appears as one of Jason's Argonauts: Bias and Melampus do not, though the latter possesses a special skill. For though the saga of the Argonauts may contain some recollections of real voyages of exploration, it also has many folk-tale motifs, one of which is a crew of Helpers, the special talents of each of whom must originally have been required. The Quest itself is such a motif: its object is the emblem of sovereignty, and not the fleece in which the Colchians collected gold-dust from a river, a rationalisation already current in antiquity.

Jason arrived at the court of Pelias

as a stranger, as the supplanter often is. But he already bore the mark of which Pelias had been warned to beware. He was the 'single-sandalled man'. This was in fact particularly an Aetolian custom, designed to give a better foothold when fighting in mud. But Jason is said to have lost the sandal when ferrying an old woman across a stream. She revealed herself as Hera and promised her help, a fairy-tale motif. Jason's absence is accounted for by the story that he had been entrusted to Chiron the Centaur for his education and safe custody, a tale told of many heroes.

The Centaurs were wild men of the Thessalian hills, lustful and easily inflamed with wine, relations of the Lapiths, whose enemies they were. They were the offspring of Ixion, whose son Pirithous was king of the Lapiths, but who seems himself to be a very primitive divine king. For he is one of those invited to Zeus' table, despite having murdered his wife's father by making him fall into a pit of burning coals when he came for the promised bride-price. Zeus purified him from this murder, which was probably originally a sacrifice.

Ixion repaid the kindness by an attempt on Hera, which was foiled when Zeus made a duplicate of her in

Jason and the snake. This cup by the great painter Douris is perhaps a little earlier than the vase depicting the Golden Fleece, but it attests Athenian interest in the myth in the early fifth century. Both vases show Jason under the protection of Athena, but this one, in which Jason is identified by name, brings out some of the ritual implications of the myth. For if Jason was swallowed and regorged by the snake it suggests that his quest was, as befits a man whose name is 'Healer', for immortality, and that he, like Pelias, died and was rejuvenated. Vases, even if they are derived from drama, often depict earlier versions of a myth than are preserved in the literary tradition. Museo Gregoriano Etrusco, Vatican.

cloud, upon which Ixion begot the first Centaur. Ixion's action was regarded as impiety and he was punished in Hades by being bound to a wheel, flaming like the pit in which his wife's father died. But Chiron, the one good Centaur, was given a different parentage, by Cronus, in the form of a horse, out of a daughter of Oceanus. Behind both these myths there seems to lie a ritual in which a god could assume the form of a horse.

The war of the Lapiths and Centaurs originated at the wedding of Pirithous, when the Centaurs got at the wine and tried to carry off the women. In the fight the invulnerable and impious Caeneus was battered into the ground by the Centaurs. Caeneus had been a woman. Poseidon raped her, and then turned her into an invulnerable man to prevent anybody from following his example. Caeneus' impiety was shown by his refusal to worship anything but his own spear stuck into the ground. Here, as in the myth of Ixion, there seems to be some primitive ritual.

Both Caeneus and Pirithous, however, appear as Argonauts, just as Jason is educated by the immortal Chiron. For despite their extremely primitive origins, the Centaurs are in the heroic tradition.

On their voyage the Argonauts met with a number of adventures, which, like all Greek mythology, contain elements of different kinds. Some may be genuine traditions from voyages of exploration; others are based on ritual, and yet others are there to enable the Helpers to display their special skills. The first stop was at Lemnos, always important because it is on the island-hopping route to the Dardanelles. Here they found only women who, 'because they did not honour Aphrodite', had been afflicted with a bad smell, which drove their husbands to fetch women from mainland Thrace. For this insult their wives killed them. There was an annual ceremony of mourning on Lemnos, during which all fires were put out for nine days, no ship might land, and the women made themselves repulsive to men with asafoetida. It was presumably part of a fertility cult, cul-

minating in an orgy such as doubtless took place when the Argonauts landed. The myth provided a historical explanation for the ceremony.

A similar ceremony lies behind the story of Hylas, the boy favourite of Heracles. He was carried off by water nymphs and vainly sought by Heracles, who 'cried "Hylas" o'er the hills', a custom annually followed in Mysia. Heracles was only attached to the expedition in order that this episode might explain the ritual. No other use is made of his special qualities. Whereas Pollux, the boxer, defeated a savage king who challenged all comers to a fight, a ritual contest which was perhaps originally held in Greece.

Similarly Zetes and Calais, winged sons of the North wind, chased away the Harpies who were persecuting the blind Phineus. In gratitude, he showed the Argonauts the way to Colchis. Phineus plays the role taken in the story of Perseus by the aged sisters. There are many sides to the Harpies, who are represented like the Sirens as birds with women's heads. They are snatching winds, or ghosts who carry off the living, but they are also like the Gorgons, and like Medusa they bear wind-swift horses to Poseidon.

The blindness of Phineus is variously explained. In the original version it was caused by the sun, either because Phineus preferred long life to sight, or because he had already revealed the way to Colchis to Phrixus. This suggests a version in which Phrixus was not the man who took the Golden Fleece to Colchis, but the man who brought it back from there, and Phineus was the guardian of the secret home of the child of the sun. The way there was further guarded by the Clashing Rocks, which even destroyed one of the doves which brought ambrosia to Zeus.

The motif of the doves is also used to explain how the *Argo* passed through these rocks, by sending out a dove which brought them together and following it through as the rocks rebounded. The doves suggest an original Quest for the Water of Life, which kept the gods immortal. The rocks have sometimes been identified as icebergs.

After arriving at Colchis, Jason had to perform traditional exploits to win the king's daughter and the Golden Fleece. The wizard's daughter, Medea, herself a witch, fell in love with him and helped him to yoke the fire-breathing bulls, sow the Dragon's teeth, and destroy the armed men who sprang up. Then she charmed the snake which guarded the Fleece, helping Jason to escape by a gruesome variant of the Flight from the Enchanter. For what she threw in the path of her father were chopped up pieces of her brother Apsyrtus, who may have started as the victim in some fertility cult.

The required exploits are paralleled and perhaps also derived from other stories. Apollo yoked a lion and boar to win Pelias' daughter for Admetus, and heroes are always dealing with monstrous bulls, lions and boars. The sown men come from the Theban legend.

The route by which the Argonauts returned was varied to accommodate increasing geographical knowledge. One way was up the river Phasis east from Colchis to Ocean, on which they turned south to the Nile, and back by Libya, colonised in the seventh century. Another route took them north and west, by the rivers Danube and Po, the old amber routes. On the way they were brought into contact with as many other myths as possible.

On his return, Jason dealt with Pelias by boiling him in a cauldron, as Ino had done to Melicertes, who became a god. Pelias was persuaded that Medea would rejuvenate him, as she did an old ram, and his daughters actually performed this task, thus removing blood-guilt from Jason. This form of sacrifice of the divine king, which is what it clearly is, seems to have been that preferred by those whose god (Zeus or Hermes) could appear in the form of a ram, the emblem of sovereignty. It recurs in the history of the house of Atreus.

The rejuvenation motif shows that, as in the case of Melicertes, the sacrifice was followed by 'resurrection', as of those heroes who were raised

from the dead by Asclepius. The magic herbs used by Medea suggest the Herb of Life found in the epic of Gilgamesh and in other Greek myths. Like the Water of Life this is often the object of a Quest to save the life of the Princess' father. The myth of Jason suggests that this Quest may not have been as beneficent and disinterested as it appears on the surface.

Pelias was succeeded by his son, whereupon Jason and Medea went to Corinth, where Jason acquired another bride in the king's daughter. But he never enjoyed her, for Medea burned her to death in a magic garment, killed her children, and fled to Athens in a chariot drawn by winged snakes. Jason died at Corinth, killed when the stern of the *Argo* fell upon him while he was asleep.

Corinth was an early and important naval city, and the Corinthians perhaps identified Jason with the hero of a local ritual. An annual ceremony mourned the slain children, and seven boys and seven girls in black with shorn hair (the Greek mark of mourning, a form of self-punitive activity) spent the year in a sanctuary, a ritual which suggests the story of the Athenian victims sent to Crete for the Minotaur. Medea may have been originally the goddess there: such fairy brides, like Thetis, always eventually desert their husbands in Greek mythology.

Jason seizing the Golden Fleece. Only two Greek vases illustrate the story of Jason and the Golden Fleece. The vase painted by the Orchard painter, about 470–460 B.C. may have been inspired by a play, possibly by Aeschylus, since it is parodied in another vase which shows a satyr playing the role of Jason under the protection of Dionysus. This vase too has a slightly comic appearance as a tiny Jason reaches up to seize the Fleece from under the head of the snake which surrounds the tree. The cloaked figure with his hand on the stern of the Argo must, from his size, be another deity, perhaps the river Phasis which is going to give the ship a good shove off to help Jason escape. The female head might be the speaking bough from Dodona built into the *Argo* where it could address the rowers. Metropolitan Museum of Art, New York, Harris Brisbane Dick Fund, 1934.

The image shows a Greek vase painting with inscriptions: ΠΕΤΡΑΙΟΣ, ΝΕΥΣ, ΗΟΠΛΟΝ, ΒΟΡΙΟΝ

Above. The battle of Lapiths and Centaurs at the wedding of Pirithous forms only one of the seven mythological friezes on the famous 'François' vase. Caeneus was being hammered into the ground to the left of this picture. The centaurs, who have by now assumed the later form of a horse body with a human torso issuing from it, are as usual armed with branches and rocks, but the Lapiths, instead of seizing what they could from the furniture of the wedding, are depicted as fully armed hoplites. The left-hand centaur is appropriately named Petraios (read from right to left), 'Rocky': the dying one (an exercise in perspective) Pyros (later Pyrrhos), 'ruddy', and by the Lapith is the word 'hoplon', 'gear' or 'equipment'. Museo Archeologico, Florence.

Opposite top. This picture by the Copenhagen painter, of about 470 B.C. on the side of a watering pot, shows a named Medea demonstrating her powers of rejuvenation by boiling a ram in a cauldron. In the stories she cut up the ram and it emerged as a lamb: in all the illustrations it is leaping from the cauldron as a rejuvenated ram. The figure on the right here, with white hair, is labelled Jason, often taken to be a mistake for his father Aeson by a painter who imagined that any man with Medea must be Jason. But Aeson committed suicide and was not rejuvenated and there is evidence that a fifth century mythographer, and also the poet Simonides, told the story about Jason – a symbolic version, modern psychologists might suppose, of the rejuvenating effect of love on an older man. British Museum, London.

Right. Medea and Pelias. The later Athenian black-figure vase painters, like the Leagros group of 530–510 B.C., had to compete with red figure, not entirely successfully. This crowded scene shows Medea at the start of her proof to Pelias that she can rejuvenate him. The ram is in the boiling cauldron, beneath which Jason adds a brand to the fire. Medea to the left looks at the aged Pelias, one of whose daughters watches in concern. The ram became a lamb. But when his daughters performed the operation on Pelias, he only became immortal perhaps, but certainly dead. British Museum, London.

Thebes

After the death of Cadmus, a second foundation story is told of Thebes, involving the divine twins Amphion and Zethus, sons of Zeus. They are the children of Antiope, who seems originally to have been the daughter of the local river Asopus. Her sons are almost completely without descendants, that is, they are outside the heroic genealogies and may have been some kind of ancient cult figures in the city of Thebes.

The only surviving descendant of the line was one of the daughters of Niobe, whom Amphion had married. Niobe likened herself to, or identified with, Leto, who, she said, had but two children, while she had six sons and six daughters. Apollo and Artemis punished this presumption by killing all the children of Niobe, 'and they lay nine days in their gore, nor was there any one to bury them; for Zeus had made the people stones'. Eventually Niobe too was turned into a stone, which still wept for its children: it was later identified with one on Mount Sipylus in Lydia, and Niobe was made daughter of Tantalus. But the story originally belonged to a Theban cult similar to that in Corinth which mourned the children of Medea. The stones suggest a stone circle, or a misapplication of the story of Deucalion, who made people from stones after the flood. The dripping stone may be a piece of water magic.

One daughter, however, is said to have been spared to marry Neleus, Pelias' brother. She became the mother of the long-lived Nestor, who was given all the years lost to his mother's kin.

Antiope is said to have been the daughter of Nycteus, who came to Thebes from Orchomenus. When she

Above. Punishment of Niobe. This masterpiece of the severe classic style of painting about 460 B.C. has given its name to the Niobid painter. The terrifying and unpitying figures of Artemis and Apollo dominate the scene as they complete the slaughter of the sons and daughters of Niobe, who dared to compare herself with Leto. Musée du Louvre, Paris.

Opposite top. The earliest, dating from the beginning of the fifth century, of a series of illustrations of Oedipus and the Sphinx. Oedipus is shown as a mature bearded traveller and the Sphinx is monumental. The scene suggests a cemetery in which a traveller meditates upon human life. Later, Oedipus appears as a young man armed with sword or spear, and the Sphinx becomes more lifelike. Musei Vaticani.

Opposite above. Oedipus slaying the Sphinx. In this late-fifth-century treatment of the myth by one of the circle of the painter Midias, Oedipus is shown in the act of killing the Sphinx. She crouches before him exposing her neck for the *coup de grâce*, as he leaps upon her with a hoplite spear. Beside the column sits Apollo, presiding over the fate of Oedipus. British Museum, London.

became pregnant, she was expelled, and in some versions she married Epopeus, king of Sicyon, from whom she was forcibly recovered by Lycus, Nycteus' brother. He imprisoned her at the instance of his wife Dirce, who hated her, and eventually proposed to kill her by tying her to the horns of a wild bull in a Dionysiac orgy on Cithaeron. From this fate she was rescued by the twins she had earlier exposed there, who had been reared by shepherds. Dirce suffered the fate she had intended for Antiope, and her dead body was thrown into a spring that took her name.

These complicated stories are the inventions of fifth-century Athenian tragedians, who habitually cast their plots into the pattern of the myth of the supplanter, elements of which they may have already attached to the stories. The three strains in Greek mythology come out very clearly in this story: the simple myth which explains a ritual, its literary elaboration with the addition of other ritual elements, and the genealogies which connected the subjects of different myths.

The best known features of the story of Amphion and Zethus come from the literary tradition. Amphion the musician is contrasted with Zethus the farmer and warrior, the former of course being preferred by the poets, who added the Orphic detail that Amphion fortified Thebes by charming the stones with his lyre. More primitive legends were attached to places: Dionysus punished Antiope for the death of his devotee, Dirce, and sent her mad to Phocis where she was buried. The tomb of her sons was at Thebes, and in the spring the Phocians tried to steal earth from it and sprinkle it on Antiope's tomb, to make their crops good and harm those of Thebes. A fertility cult lies behind this survival; but it may not have been originally attached to Amphion and Zethus and their mother.

Oedipus

The great Theban dynasty was that of the Labdacids, to which Oedipus belonged. Labdacus, founder of the line, is only artifically linked to the

house of Cadmus, but his mother is the daughter of one of the Sown men. In all Theban myths the inheritance in the female line is much clearer than it is in any other stories, perhaps because the myths are older. Nycteus and Lycus, and Amphion and Zethus, are fitted in as regents or usurpers, Nycteus sometimes as one of the Sown men himself. Labdacus has no mythology and may be only a cipher: his name suggests the Greek letter lambda, 'L'. Laius, Oedipus' father, is sent into exile to Elis, where he carried off Pelops' son while teaching him to drive a chariot. Pelop's curses were the cause of the fate of the Labdacids. The homosexuality theme must be late: Laius behaves as a typical supplanter, like Pelops, and suffers, again while driving a chariot, the same fate himself.

The oracle warned Laius that he would die at the hands of his son: in consequence, his child was exposed on Cithaeron with his feet pinned together by a spike. But the child was

found by shepherds of the childless king of Corinth, Polybus, who reared the child as his own and called him Oedipus, 'Swell-foot', because of his mutilation. Grown to manhood, Oedipus was taunted by a drunk with not being the true son of his father, and himself went to the oracle at Delphi for information, only to be told that he would marry his mother and kill his father. Resolved never to return to Corinth, he set out for Thebes. He was forced from the road by an old man in a waggon, whom he killed. He found Thebes beset by the Sphinx (the Strangler) whose riddle he was able to solve, becoming king in place of Laius, who had been killed by robbers on a journey. Oedipus then married the queen, Jocasta, who bore him two sons and two daughters.

It is possible to see how at some time the myth of Oedipus was modified to create a motif of incest and parricide which may have been absent in its original form. For the Oedipus story is created by combining the two forms of the story of the supplanter. In one, Oedipus is the stranger who performs the exploit of defeating the Sphinx and is thus chosen to marry the queen (or the king's daughter) and inherit the kingdom: in the other, he is the divinely begotten grandson, the grand-daughter's husband who becomes king. It is the combination of the two which gives the situation of Oedipus its particular horror. The incest motif is normally absent, and that of parricide is disguised by making the child the son of a god, the murdered father a grandfather or uncle, and the murder itself no more than an accident.

When Oedipus discovered he had killed his father and married his mother, Jocasta committed suicide and Oedipus blinded himself. His wife's brother, the important figure in matrilinear societies, ruled in Thebes until Oedipus' sons, Eteocles and Polynices, came of age, when they quarrelled over the joint kingship, as if they were twins. Oedipus cursed them and went to Athens, where his buried corpse defended the frontier against the Thebans who had rejected him. Polynices went into exile to Argos, where he married the daughter of Adrastus the king. Adrastus had been told to yoke his daughters to the lion and the boar, and he recognised in Polynices the lion. For he bore that Theban emblem on his shield.

The Seven against Thebes

This is the occasion of the next great communal enterprise of the Heroic Age, the two attacks on Thebes by the Seven and their sons. It seems to be genuine saga, reflecting political rivalry between Argos and Thebes. Hesiod says that some of the heroes died at Thebes fighting for the sheep of Oedipus. In the epic tradition the first attack may have been made in the lifetime of Oedipus, and be the cause of his death and the last evil brought upon him by the Furies invoked by his mother's curse.

The attack was led from Argos in the interests of a Theban pretender. But there was a Calydonian contingent which links this communal exploit with that of the Calydonian Boar hunt. Tydeus, son of Oeneus, was also in exile for killing some close male relative. He married the other daughter of Adrastus: for on his shield was emblazoned the Calydonian Boar.

Atalanta's son Parthenopaeus also joined the attack on Thebes, as an Arcadian rather than a Boeotian, and the tomb of Oecles, father of the reluctant seer Amphiaraus, was also shown in Arcadia. Amphiaraus was reluctant to join the attack because he knew that, like so many of these communal enterprises, it was bound to fail. But his wife, Eriphyle, was bribed with the necklace of Harmonia and she sent her husband to his death. In fact, Amphiaraus was probably bound by the rule of a matrilinear society to follow Adrastus who was his wife's brother.

On their way to Thebes the Seven founded the Isthmian games, in honour of Opheltes Archemorus, the Corinthian king's infant son, devoured by a serpent when his nurse showed the Seven a spring. His name suggests that he was himself a snake, Ruler of Death, and the object of a local cult. The games, of course, commemorate a dead man as well as selecting his supplanter.

Amphiaraus also received cult as an oracular hero when Zeus opened a cleft in the earth with a thunderbolt before him as he fled from Thebes defeated, and he vanished down it. In the fifth century the Thebans transferred the cult to the border town of Oropus, of which they disputed possession with the Athenians, in order that the oracular hero might protect the frontier.

All the Seven died except Adrastus, who escaped on his magic horse Arion. Tydeus was invited alone into Thebes, beat them all at athletic contests, and then slew all but one of a fifty-man ambush on the way back. This suggests an exploit, like that of Bellerophon. In the attack of the Seven, which the Thebans repulsed by sacrificing the son of king Creon, Tydeus was fatally wounded by Melanippus, who was also killed. Athena would have made Tydeus immortal, but he disgusted her by eating the brains of his dead adversary before he died, an act of ritual cannibalism which may originally have been the very means of immortality.

Polynices fought Eteocles, his brother, at one of the seven gates of Thebes. Both were killed, but Polynices was left to rot unburied on the orders of Creon. Antigone disobeyed his orders, for her brother Polynices was more important to her than husband or child would have been. Antigone was walled up in a cave to die without polluting her killers: Creon's son died with her, for love.

The Theban victory had been what the Greeks called a Cadmean victory, which like a Pyrrhic victory was too costly to the winners. Ten years later the sons of the Seven succeeded in restoring Thersander, Polynices' son. This time victory was promised them under the leadership of Alcmaeon, son of Amphiaraus, who defeated the Thebans in a pitched battle at Glisas where their tombs were shown. Then Tiresias advised them to abandon Thebes, and they went out in waggons and joined the tribe of the Illyrians to which Cadmus and Harmonia had gone before.

Above. The sixth-century temple C at Selinus stood on the Acropolis on the edge of the sea, to the west of the ancient port in the estuary. Only the north side of the temple has been rebuilt: it collapsed early in the Christian era, when Selinus was a decayed village. The photograph shows it from the inside. The entrance was to the right, and the surviving metopes were on its façade.

Opposite. Archaic Etruscan gems, from the turn of the sixth/fifth centuries B.C., favoured as subjects a single usually nude and male figure drawn from Greek mythology and depicted in the muscular style of the Greek sculpture of the period. The one on the left clearly depicts Ixion on his wheel, which has been made oval to accommodate the shape of the gem, and is also inscribed with his name. But the details of the legend are forgotten: Ixion appears almost as a Prometheus figure, a noble hero unjustly suffering. The one on the right depicts Sisyphus pushing his stone up a hill. British Museum, London.

Not all late Roman carving is equally successful as art, and many later sarcophagi can be dreary and fussy. But this alabaster urn from Chiusi, which is plausibly identified as the dying Eteocles and Polynices, combines the two figures, in identical but reversed postures, in a scene of tremendous emotional power, which is enhanced by the presence of the winged figure (possibly the curse of Oedipus) staring directly out with almost Byzantine intensity. In earlier ancient accounts, it is the impiety of the brothers, especially of Polynices, that is stressed: here the pathos of brother killing brother is much stronger. It was a theme known to the Roman experience from their frequent civil wars, fought largely by a professional army which often contained relatives, who found themselves on opposite sides. Museo Archaeologico, Florence.

Tiresias, the Theban prophet, appears in every Greek tragedy set in Thebes, from the *Bacchae* to the *Antigone*. He was already famous enough for Odysseus to make a special, but unnecessary, journey to Hades to get from him information which Circe also gave him: for he was the only man to retain his intelligence among the dead. He was a nymph's son, given the gift of prophecy when he was blinded for seeing Athena naked, a legend that may have been deliberately modelled on that of Actaeon.

In what is probably the earlier legend Tiresias saw and disturbed two snakes coupling, and was turned into a woman. This enabled him to settle a quarrel between Zeus and Hera by testifying from personal experience that in love a man enjoys only a tenth of the woman's pleasure. This assertion, part of a patriarchal society's resentment and envy of women, so angered Hera by its revelation of women's secrets that in revenge she turned Tiresias back into a man, or else he saw and disturbed the same snakes again.

Tiresias finally died when Thebes was evacuated. His daughter was sent to Delphi, to which the Argives had vowed the fairest of the spoils. This looks like a variant of the common motif of the home-comer's vow. Alcmaeon returned home and avenged his father's death by killing his mother, for which the Furies drove him mad. Exile to Psophis, with marriage to the king's daughter, did not cure him: instead, the earth refused to bear fruit. Finally he settled on a land that had not existed when he did the deed, the islands freshly laid down at the mouth of the river Achelous. This literal approach is found also in the story of the birth of Apollo and Artemis on Delos.

Alcmaeon married the river's daughter, Callirhoe, who wanted the necklace of Harmonia which Alcmaeon had given to Arsinoe. He asked for it back, pretending he was going to dedicate it at Delphi, but his wife's brothers discovered the deception and murdered him. Callirhoe then prayed that her infant sons, whose father may have been Zeus, might at once become full grown to avenge Alcmaeon's death. This they did, and took the necklace at last to Delphi.

There are early and late elements in this story, which was dramatised by both Sophocles and Euripides. The Delphic oracle is late. But the swift-growing children are giants like Otus and Ephialtes, and the role of the wife's brother belongs to matrilinear society. Matricide is the crime of a patriarchal society, in which a wife's infidelity is to be punished with death.

The stories of the two great matricides, Alcmaeon and Orestes, although they may have influenced one another, may, like the stories in which gods strive for possession of a land, reflect the conflict between patriarchal and matrilinear societies and their respective rituals and customs.

Heracles

The story of Heracles is another that connects Thebes and Argos. But this is because a Tirynthian hero, a descendant of Perseus in the junior line and vassal of the lord of Mycenae, has been identified with a Theban hero called Alcaeus, 'Mighty'. To his story have been added folk-tales of a strong man of insatiable appetites, capable of fathering fifty sons in a night.

Amphitryon

Amphitryon, Heracles' father, went from Argos to Thebes in a typical story of exile. Perseus' grand-daughter Hippothoe, 'Swift Mare', was carried off by Poseidon and bore him Pterelaus, king of the Teleboans, whom his father made immortal by putting his external soul into a golden hair on his head. If he was blond it was indistinguishable from the rest, and it is clear that only his daughter knew which one it was. In the genealogies, Poseidon's son is called Taphius, but he is inserted only to identify the Teleboans with an existing tribe: the golden hair shows that Pterelaus was originally the god's son.

Pterelaus' sons claimed Mycenae from their mother's uncle, Electryon, who went off to fight them. He left his kingdom, his cattle and his daughter to his wife's brother Amphitryon, making him swear to respect Alcmena's virginity. But when Electryon got back Amphitryon killed him in an 'accident': his club bounced off the horns of a charging cow. So Amphitryon went to Thebes and the fourth son of Perseus, Eurystheus, took over Mycenae.

In Thebes, too, Amphitryon behaved like a typical supplanter. First he delivered the land from a monstrous vixen which could never be

Top. Reverse of Syracusian gold 100 litra piece, 390–380 B.C. Heracles wrestles with the Nemean lion whose skin he later wore.

Above. Reverse of stater from Croton about 350 B.C.. In the fourth century the youthful Heracles, resting after a labour, was replaced on coins by the child strangling the snakes sent against him by Hera. Private collection.

caught. It had been sent by Dionysus and children had to be exposed to it. Amphitryon sent against it a wonderful hound like that with which Phylacus guarded his cattle. It never failed of its quarry, and the gods resolved this folk-tale dilemma by turning them both to stone, probably a pair of standing stones.

Then Amphitryon resumed the war against the Teleboans, because

Alcmena, with proper matrilinear piety, refused to yield her virginity until he had avenged the death of her brothers, killed in the previous war. Pterelaus' daughter Comaetho fell in love with Amphitryon and killed her father by pulling out the golden hair to which her name refers (*comé* = hair). By all the rules Amphitryon should have married her: instead, like a good patriarchal hero, he killed her for her treachery and returned to Alcmena. But he found that he had been anticipated by Zeus, who had taken his form and prolonged the night to the length of three to beget the mighty Heracles. Amphitryon then begot the mortal twin, Iphicles.

Birth of Heracles

When Heracles was to be born, Zeus vowed that the next Perseid born should rule Mycenae, intending it to be Heracles. But Hera sent Ilithyia, who presided over childbirth, to stop the birth by sitting cross-legged, a

common piece of magic, until Sthenelus' wife bore Eurystheus as a seven-month child. Ilithyia did not go away until somebody gave a cry of joy as if Alcmena had been delivered, which she then was. This story was told to explain how it was that the mighty Heracles had to serve Eurystheus, just as the complicated series of perhaps traditional tales about Amphitryon were used to get Heracles born in Thebes in the period after the death of Oedipus. But Heracles' position may really reflect the political fact that Tiryns was subordinate to Mycenae.

Heracles was eventually admitted to Olympus and became the object of cult, though only rarely as a god, mostly as a kind of very superior hero. A legend was told to show how he was prepared for his fate in infancy. At the same time it brings him into filial relation with Hera, whose name he bears, though in the developed legend she is his implacable

enemy. Zeus lulled Hera asleep, and Hermes put Heracles to her breast: but he bit it and awoke her, and she thrust him off, spilling her milk over the firmament as the Milky Way. This has the appearance of a late Alexandrian myth. Hera also sent snakes to the cradle of the twins: Iphicles is shown on a vase painting as cowering, while Heracles strangled them.

The Exploits of Heracles

Heracles' earliest exploits are located at Thebes. At eighteen he killed the lion of Cithaeron, whose skin he always wore, and begot fifty sons in one night on the fifty daughters of Thespius. He won one of them. Thespius fed the others in to him in relays, though he thought it was always the same one. He also won Creon's daughter, as a reward for delivering the Thebans from a tribute paid to Orchomenus, perhaps a genuine piece of historical information. But he went mad and killed his children and so was sent to perform Labours for Eurystheus in penance. Thus again a variation on a traditional theme was used to get Heracles back to Argos.

But Alcmena, who was probably originally a name or title of a mother-goddess, remained located at Thebes, where two curious legends were told about her. One tells how Amphitryon condemned her to be burnt to death for her supposed infidelity when he was fighting the Teleboans. But Zeus extinguished the pyre with a miraculous shower of rain, perhaps originally a piece of rain magic. The other legend tells how Hermes stole her from the bier when she was dead, and substituted a stone which the Thebans reverenced, while Zeus took her to the Isles of the Blessed. This is partly an aetiological myth, partly the result of a feeling that the mother of Heracles deserved special treatment.

Almost all Heracles' Labours are variants of the single exploit by which the hero vanquishes a monster. The first five are all localised in the Peloponnese: the Nemean lion, the Lernaean hydra, the Ceryneian hind with its golden horns, the Erymanthian boar, and the Stymphalian birds. To all of these various other legends are attached. To deal with the hydra, which had nine heads, each of which was replaced by two when it was cut off, Heracles enlisted the help of Iolaus, but only because Hera sent a crab to bite his heel and 'even Heracles cannot fight two' as the Greek proverb said. Iolaus seared the roots with fire as each head was cut off.

With the hydra's poison Heracles anointed the arrows of the bow with which, exceptionally for a hero, he was normally armed and not with the traditional club. With these arrows he drove off the drunken Centaurs with whom he lodged when fetching the boar. He accidentally wounded Chiron, who traded his immortality with the Titan Prometheus (another late legend, for Titans normally seem to be immortal). The birds he scared with brazen castanets made by Hephaestus.

Some of Heracles' other Labours are also single exploits. He overcame the Cretan Bull, a sacred animal, which was either that which carried Europa or one sent out of the sea by Poseidon. He also tamed the man-eating Mares of Diomede of Thrace, captured the Cattle of Geryon, and even brought up the three-headed dog Cerberus from Hades. Diomede was a son of Ares, and so might be expected to have used his mares to race the suitors of his daughters, and then to tear them apart, possibly in honour of Dionysus. This motif has been suppressed in the interest of Heracles. But a son of Hermes was dragged to

death by the mares when Heracles left them with him.

The Quests of Heracles

The other Labours are quests, which took Heracles progressively further afield and even outside the world of men. One of the Peloponnesian Labours may have started as a quest, the cleansing of the cowsheds of Augeas, which Heracles accomplished by diverting a river. For Augeas in some versions was the child of the Sun and the task is of the type of impossible ones which have to be performed to win the Magician's daughter. In a fairy tale it would be done for him by animals which he had befriended. More prosaically, the Labour has elements of a simple cattle raid. So has

Opposite left. Heracles and the Erymanthian boar. Heracles is presenting the boar head down to a completely terrified Eurystheus who cowers in a huge pithos buried almost to the neck in the earth. Athena on one side stretches

out her left hand, beautifully extending the aegis fringed with snakes. On the other side a bearded Iolaus holds the club (the bow and arrows are on Heracles' back). British Museum, London.

Opposite right. Heracles with his family. The decorations on oil-flasks are often either sepulchral or domestic, reflecting their two chief uses. The genre scene of the son reaching out for his father from his mother's lap is given piquancy by its application to Heracles, not the most domestic of heroes. He is resting on his club with his bow probably unstrung and strapped to the quiver. His wife Deianeira holds their son Hyllus, who survived Heracles to become the ancestor of the Dorians. Ashmolean Museum, Oxford.

Below. Heracles and the Centaurs. The city of Assos occupies an impregnable site on the mainland of Asia Minor opposite the island of Lesbos, and was the first site ever to be excavated by the American Institute of Archaeology. A late-sixth-century temple was found there. Following Ionian practice, the architrave immediately above the columns was sculptured as well as the metopes, while the pediment was left bare. The hard volcanic stone partly accounts for the primitive appearance of this relief, which shows Heracles with his bow driving off the Centaurs. While seeking the Erymanthian boar he lodged in Arcadia

with Pholus, seen on the left with a cup of the wine which he specially opened for Heracles. The wine maddened the Centaurs, and they attacked Heracles. Museum of Fine Arts, Boston. Gift of the Archeological Institute of America.

Bottom left. Heracles and the Stymphalian birds. Heracles was always one of the most popular subjects of Attic vase painting, and especially so in the sixth century, when Athens was still strongly aristocratic. In this amphora by a predecessor of the great master Exekias, about 560 B.C., Heracles is attacking the Symphalian birds with a sling. British Museum, London.

Bottom right. The technique of red-figure painting, which allowed the artist to put in details on the figures, was discovered about 530 B.C. Around 510 both painter Euphronius and potter Cachrylion signed a cup on the outside of which Heracles' exploit against Geryon is shown. Heracles, having used his bow to kill the three-headed hound and one of the bodies of Geryon, advances with his club on the other two. Geryon looks like three hoplites in line: two shield emblems can be seen, a winged pig and an octopus. Athena, with the gorgon on her shield, hastens to his aid, leaving Iolaus and the wounded Eurytion in reserve. Staatliche Antikensammlungen und Glyptothek, Munich.

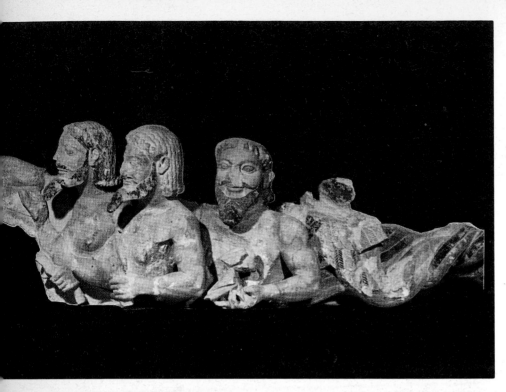

Left. The decoration of the pediment of a Greek temple presented a number of problems to the sculptor who wished to create a unified scheme. One of the greatest was how to fill the two sides where they slope to a narrow point. In the old Athena temple, associated with the tyrant Pisistratus and dating probably from about 560 B.C., these spaces were filled by monstrous figures, which could easily be adapted to any area. At one end Heracles wrestled with a Triton. At the other appeared this three-bodied serpent man with wings. Benevolent though he looks, such three-bodied figures are in mythology almost always hostile, and he could possibly be another opponent of Heracles, even Geryon himself. Acropolis Museum, Athens.

Opposite. Heracles bringing Cerberus to Eurystheus. This fine example of the highly coloured and slightly comic painting of the Ionian emigrant who decorated vases at Caere was discovered unbroken, presumably in the tomb in which it was buried with its owner. The artist has chosen to show Eurystheus cowering in a large pot before the latest monster Heracles has brought back. This motif is more usually combined with the exploit of the Erymanthian boar. Cerberus is more often shown being enticed by Heracles with the help of Athena. All three heads are shown by this literal minded painter, each distinguished by colour. Nine snakes grow from him, to indicate his infernal origin, three for each head. One snake survives in later two-headed representations. Musée du Louvre, Paris.

Left. Heracles again employs his club and almost, it seems, the tripod in this late and rather clumsy vase in which Apollo's right arm is badly out of drawing and scale, but which has a certain dramatic vigour. The following of a single illustrated theme through a number of representations in different media can tell more about the history of art and myth in Greece than many words. British Museum, London.

that of the Cattle of Geryon, the three-bodied giant. But he lived beyond Ocean, on which Heracles sailed in the Sun's Golden Bowl. He got the Bowl by threatening to shoot the Sun with his arrows, and when Ocean tried to swamp it, he threatened him too. These are the acts of the god in a succession myth, and the cattle, even if originally those of the Sun, are not entirely in place, though Apollodorus solemnly has Heracles embark them too in the Bowl to bring them back.

A slightly more traditional quest is that for the Girdle of Hippolyta, the Amazon Queen, who yielded it to him willingly. It was given to Hippolyta by Ares because of the warlike prowess of the Amazons, who lived without men and met their neighbours only once a year for procreation. They reared only the girls, cutting off the right breast so that it should not get in the way when they drew the bow-string or threw the spear, a detail usually ignored in art. Whatever their origin in beardless oriental warriors, the Amazons are a male fantasy of role reversal, and are extremely popular in art.

In another legend, Heracles served Omphale, a Lydian Queen, for three years in expiation for a murder, during which time he wore women's dress, perhaps to deceive the ghost. The episode with the Amazons looks like a variant of this. It may have been borrowed from the myth of Theseus, who plays an important part in the war that Hera is said to have stirred up, though such borrowings are usually the other way round. Little is made of the Labour, except to provide an opportunity for Heracles' visits to Troy, and to make up the canonical number of Labours.

These were originally ten, all of which, including the contests with monsters, have this much of the quest about them that Heracles brings all the objects back to Eurystheus, who cowers in terror in a brazen pot which he buries in the earth. Later the canon was made up to twelve by the addition of two more which are much more other-wordly. Eurystheus is said to have rejected two of the Labours,

Below. The third metope from the temple of Hera at Selinus shows Heracles about to kill the Amazon Queen Hippolyta. She had promised to yield him her girdle willingly, but Hera provoked the other Amazons into an attack. The ambiguities of love and death contained in this legend fascinated the artists of the Periclean period. Heracles uses his lion skin as a shield to ward off the axe blows of the Amazon, and seizes her oriental helmet as he prepares the *coup de grâce* with his club (now lost). Museo Nazionale, Palermo.

Opposite top. Heracles in the garden of the Hesperides. The Athenian vase painter Midias, at the end of the fifth century, decorated a water pot with two bands, one on the shoulder and one below the handle. In the centre of the latter Heracles is sitting on his lion skin

on a rock in the garden of the Hesperides. He is looking at one of them named Lipara 'shining', who already holds an apple. Behind Heracles is his squire Iolaus, and the garden is full of Argonauts (not shown in this detail). British Museum, London.

Bottom right. Heracles and the Golden Apples of the Hesperides. The sculptured metopes of the early-fifth-century temple of Zeus at Olympia were not under the pediment, but over the porches in front of and behind the shrine. Twelve in number, they seem to have shown the Twelve Labours of Heracles, founder of the Olympian games and the great hero of the Dorians, who developed the games during the eighth century. Heracles did not get the Golden Apples of the Hesperides himself. The giant Atlas got them for him while Heracles supported the vault of heaven on a cushion. Athena, shown here as a severe maiden, helped him, taking the weight with her left hand. At this period, the hero is clearly inferior to the gods. Archaeological Museum, Olympia.

Above. Siphnos, in the Cyclades, was, in the time of Polycrates of Samos, about 520 B.C., the richest of the islands because of its mines of gold and silver, of which the inhabitants dedicated a tithe to Apollo, and built a treasury (a small temple in form) to house it. When they omitted the tithe, it was said, the mines were flooded (more probably in fact it was the other way round, but the story was told to enhance the power of Delphi). Their treasury was the most lavishly decorated of all at Delphi, since they could afford to pay the best artists. The frieze shows the goddesses arriving in their chariots for the judgement of Paris, and also a Gigantomachy, the battle of the gods and giants, from which this illustration is taken. The gods are to be recognised by their attributes: here Apollo and Artemis, assisted by Ares who is dressed as a hoplite, attack the phalanx of giants, also shown as hoplites, and advance over a dead giant. Behind them, one of the lions that draw the chariot of Rhea, the mother of the gods (later identified with the Asia Minor goddess Cybele) attacks another giant. Archaeological Museum, Delphi.

the Cowsheds of Augeas and the Lernean hydra, the one because it was done for pay and the other because Heracles had help.

First Heracles was sent for the Golden Apples of the Hesperides, perhaps a variant of the Water of Life with the same sinister implications. For a moment Heracles plays the part of the giant who bears heaven and earth, taking over that burden from Atlas, who fetched him the apples. He made Atlas take it back by a trick, saying that he would fetch a pad and return, the motif of the Trickster. This myth is the origin of the pillars of Heracles, from which, wreathed with the snake that guarded the apples, the dollar sign is derived. They were transferred to the story of Geryon, located in Spain, where the symbol was often used on coins.

After this Heracles went to Hades to bring back the dog Cerberus, whose three heads suggest that Geryon also, with his three bodies, really lived there too. A number of Greek heroes, and the god Dionysus, 'harrow hell' in this way. The story seems to contain a number of themes: the Quest for the Water of Life, the Death and Resurrection of the Hero, and the Return of the Girl in the Spring, the last appearing in the story of Alcestis.

Heracles' other adventures are closer to the traditional pattern of the supplanter, suggesting that he has been identified with a number of local heroes. First he gave his wife Megara to Iolaus, his assistant, and wooed Iole, daughter of Eurytus, beating her father at archery. When Eurytus refused to pay up, on the reasonable grounds that Heracles might go mad

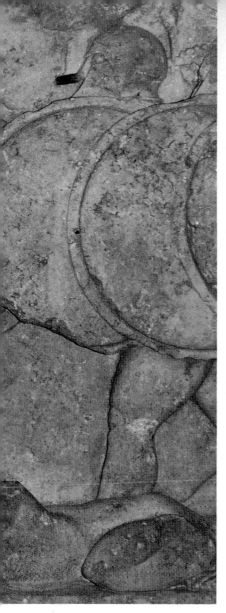

Below. Heracles bringing Cerberus from the underworld. The type of the youthful Heracles was known as early as the end of the sixth century, and appears in this plate by Paseas, who has simply applied to the circular area at his disposal part of a frieze of figures, filling the bottom with a palmette. Aided by Hermes, who conducts men to the underworld and is identified by the caduceus and hat, Heracles, waving his bow and dressed in an apparently headless lion skin, leads up Cerberus. Museum of Fine Arts, Boston, Massachusetts. Pierce Fund.

again and kill his children, Heracles killed Eurytus' son and went to Delphi to be purified. There he was involved in a fight with Apollo over the Tripod. This suggests that Apollo may have been originally involved in some way in the contest for the daughter of Eurytus, who was, like him, an archer. This is the context of Heracles' service with Omphale, which provides also the occasion for his second visit to Troy, where his role, to be discussed with the other Trojan stories, was originally that of a supplanter.

The Battle of the Gods and Giants

On his return from Troy, Heracles was co-opted as the gods' Helper in their fight with the Giants, who could be defeated only by a mortal. The Giants, born of Earth by the blood of Uranus, belong to the succession myth. But, like Otus and Ephialtes, they have been transferred to the time of the heroes in order to make use of Heracles. One early motif survives. There was a herb which would make the Giants completely immortal (obviously the Herb of Life): but Zeus forbade Sun and Moon to shine, and picked the herb himself, to stop Earth getting it.

The succession myth and the myth of the supplanter are in fact the same story appearing in a divine and in a human context. The human may have impersonated the god, as many heroes are explicitly punished for doing. If so, the myth originated in ritual, though it continued to be told because of the psychological satisfaction it provided. Elements of it were therefore added to other mythical stories, all of which show a tendency to fall into that archetypal pattern. It seems very possible that such a ritual of succession was at some time carried out at least at some places in Greece.

Two of the Giants perform deeds that recur in other myths: Alcyoneus stole the cattle of the Sun, and Porphyrion tried to rape Hera. They were defeated on the Phlegraean plains in Thessaly, near Mount Olympus. But Heracles' position is ambiguous, because at Pylos, where he slew all the descendants of Neleus except Nestor, he fought with the gods, wounding Hades with his arrows, hitting Hera in her right breast, and gashing Ares in the thigh. Pylos seems to have been an entrance to the Underworld, but Heracles is behaving like a Giant.

But most of his opponents are Giants, who keep on turning up in his

Above. The story of Heracles and Old Age is a folk tale known only from art and not from literature. Several vases show Heracles in all his accoutrements attacking a dwarf figure labelled 'Old Age'. This Etruscan bronze mirror, the other side of which was originally highly polished, may show an idealised version, perhaps derived from a comedy, in which 'Old Age' was a giant. Museum of Fine Arts, Boston, Massachusetts.

Above left. Another metope from the late-sixth-century temple C at Selinus shows Heracles with the two Cercopes. These mischievous monkey men stole Heracles' bow as he slept on a rock at Thermopylae. But when he woke, he caught them and hung them upside down on a pole over his shoulders. In that position they had a good view of his hairy rump and they recognised the black bottom of which their mother had warned them to beware. Museo Nazionale, Palermo.

Left. This late (about 410 B.C.) and vigorous painting of Heracles rescuing Deianeira from the Centaur Nessus is an exact copy of a vase signed by both potter and painter, Erginus and Aristophanes. In earlier versions Heracles has the lion skin, but he is always armed with the club, though in the literary tradition he used his arrows, the poison from which turned Nessus' blood into the charm that caused Heracles' death. Museum of Fine Arts, Boston, Massachusetts. Pierce Fund.

stories. One of the most famous is Antaeus, who regained his strength when he touched his mother, the Earth, and was dealt with by being held in the air until he died. A pair of divine twins, sons of Poseidon, were turned into a two-bodied giant called 'the Molione'. He also overthrew an Egyptian king who practised human sacrifice and tried it on Heracles.

The Death of Heracles

Finally Heracles himself met his fate, at the hands of a woman and a dead man. He wrestled with the river Achelous, who took the form of a bull-headed snake, for the hand of Deianeira. But he took her into exile because he committed another 'accidental' murder at the wedding: it was said to be that of a cup-bearer, but must have been originally the father of the bride. On the way the centaur Nessus carried Deianeira across a river and then he tried to rape her. Heracles killed him with his poisoned arrows, but, before he died, he gave Deianeira a charm to keep her husband's love. She used it when Heracles sacked the city of Eurytus and sent back Iole as his prize. But Nessus' charm, his blood with which she was to anoint a garment (the Shirt of Nessus), was in fact a poison which burned him up, similar to that which Medea gave to Jason's intended bride. Like that, it is a magic equivalent of the pyre upon which Heracles, recognising and consenting to his fate, immolated himself on Mount Oeta. He handed on to the man who lit the pyre his magic bow and arrows which were the symbols of his sovereignty.

There is a folk-tale motif in this story partly explicit and partly implicit. It was Heracles' fate to die at the hands of no man living, a literal ambiguity. It may have originally meant at the hands of the supplanter who brought the Water or Herb of Life from the land of the dead. But in the story it means at the hand of a dead man. Deianeira's willingness to employ the charm may have been similarly explained if Nessus told her that, when it was used, Heracles would never love another woman.

The death of all heroes may once

have meant their immortality. In Heracles the theme is made explicit, and he ascends to Olympus from the pyre in the form of an eagle, the bird of Zeus whose son he was. There he was reconciled to Hera, possibly his original mother, given eternal youth, and Hebe, the cupbearer of the gods, to wed. But on earth he never received divine honours, only those paid to heroes. In Greek theology the race of gods and the race of men, though born of a single mother, were always separate, and woe betide any mortal who tried to overstep the bounds of his mortality.

Heracles and the tripod of Delphi. One of the earliest surviving vases in the red-figure technique, by the Andocides painter, shows the fight between Apollo and Heracles for the tripod of Delphi. When Heracles killed the son of Eurytus, who refused him his daughter, he went to Delphi to be purified. When the Pythia, the priestess, refused, Heracles stole the tripod and carried it off with the approval of Athena. Staatliche Museen, Antikenabteilung, Berlin.

Above. Vases sometimes provide almost the only evidence for a myth and sometimes vary the details of a well-known one in a way which can make identification difficult. Here Heracles is easily recognised, as usual, by his club and lion skin (though he has a sword and not a bow). The female figure, whose hand is restrained by Poseidon, who holds his trident, is less easily named. She is wearing a goat skin, with the horned head forming a helmet, and this has led to her identification as Hera, whom Heracles wounded in the breast at Pylos (but with an arrow, and with Ares

and Hades, according to a mythological passage in the *Iliad*.) Another interpretation might be that the goat skin is the aegis, and the figure Athena, who is not attacking Heracles but joining him in an attack on the cauldron of snakes. The latter might be an offbeat representation of the Hydra, which lived in the springs of Amymone (a daughter of Danaus loved by Poseidon) who might be the female figure behind Heracles, and who would account for the presence of Poseidon. The vase still awaits final explanation. British Museum London.

Opposite. Heracles, again nude, but bearded and somewhat wild in appearance, is easily identifiable by his club and bow in this black-figure watering-pot. He is attacking an even wilder giant, who sits on the ground, in part to accommodate him to the vase while showing his size. But he may well be Alcyoneus, whom Heracles killed in the battle with the Giants, and who gained strength when he touched his native soil, and had to be dragged off the battlefield to die. Musei Vaticani.

Athens

Geographically, Attica, that is the eastward-facing peninsula in mainland Greece, has always been one of the poorer and less important regions of Greece. It does not even lie on the main line of communications between Boeotia and the Peloponnese, which passes through Corinth. Though Athens was a Mycenaean settlement, the isolation of Attica, which also preserved it from disturbance, is reflected in the comparative paucity of Attic mythology. The later importance of Athens was based on sea power, protecting the export of olive oil, wine, pottery and silver which paid for the imported corn necessary to feed a swollen manufacturing population. This policy, and the religious and political unification of Attica, was fostered, with popular support against the aristocracy, by the 'tyrant' Pisistratus, who could cast himself as the special favourite of Athena, whose Panathenaic festival he created. Much of the Athenian mythology, including that of Theseus, bears the mark of this period. None the less,

the Piraeus, the harbour of Athens, is well situated not only for trading with the Black sea, the granary of Athens, but also with the south and east. So the links of Athenian mythology with Crete may indeed go back to an earlier period. As Schliemann followed Homer to Troy and to Mycenae, so Sir Arthur Evans was led by the myth of Theseus and the Minotaur to discover the centre of the great Minoan civilisation at Cnossus.

The first inhabitant of Attica was an earthborn serpent-man called Cecrops. He was the judge in the contest between Athena and Poseidon for

The temple of Athena Nike ('Victory') stands on the site of an old Mycenaean bastion which covered the entrance to the Acropolis and enabled the defenders to throw at the unprotected right side of the attackers. It was an appropriate site for such a shrine, and as early as 449 B.C. there were plans to build a temple to commemorate the role of the goddess in the victories of the Persian War. But they interfered with Pericles' designs for the Propylaea and were not carried out until 421 B.C.

Below. Agrigento, the ancient Acragas, was founded early in the sixth century from Gela to extend Greek control westwards on the south coast of Sicily. After the defeat of the Cathaginians in 480 B.C. an aggressive democracy turned the acropolis into a monumental display of power, with a huge temple of Zeus flanked by five temples along the city wall. Of these, Temple F, seen here from the north-east, is contemporary with the Parthenon but older in style.

Bottom. The Parthenon was built at Athens under Pericles in the 440s B.C. on the site of an earlier temple destroyed by the Persians. The Athenians used some of the money paid as tribute by the Greek islands for defence against the Persians, and deliberately constructed on the Acropolis a monumental display of the power of Athens that had kept the Persians out of the Aegean. The western façade of the Parthenon, shown here, was that seen from the entrance porch.

The sculptures on the pediment showed the conflict of Athena and Poseidon for the land of Attica, but only the figures of Cecrops and one of his daughters are left on the temple. The metopes below, which are still in place, showed the battle of the Athenians and Amazons. The processional way from the entrance led round to the eastern end of the Parthenon, from which the shrine was entered which housed the huge gold and ivory statue of Athena.

Left. The goddess Athena as Defender of the City, Promachos, she who fights for it, is naturally associated strongly with Athens, the city from which the goddess in fact takes her name. Pericles set up a colossal bronze statue of the goddess in this pose beside the Parthenon as part of his redevelopment of the Acropolis. It was reproduced in large numbers of small votive statues of varying date and competence, and copied over much of the Greek and Roman world. In her left hand she holds a hoplite shield, almost horizontal to keep the opponent at as great a distance as possible, while she threatens him with the stabbing spear held in the right. The goddess dispenses with the breastplate, instead of which she sometimes wears the aegis, or divine goatskin with the gorgon's head. But she is normally helmeted. This version, in which the high plume suggests Italy, has a certain coarse strength about it. British Museum, London.

Opposite. The legend of Theseus may well reflect the real unification of Attica under the progressive tyrant Pisistratus, who claimed to have returned under the special protection of Athena. But Athena was also the patron of the democracy that followed the tyranny. The aristocrats too, who falsely claimed to have overthrown the tyranny (which was really done by the Spartans) could also lay claim to Athena, as is shown by this prize vase given at the Panathenaic festival which had been introduced, or elaborated by Pisistratus. For the shield blazon of Athena is the well-known group of the two aristocratic tyrannicides. The vase shows how art could be used for political propaganda in Athens. British Museum, London.

possession of the land, and awarded it to Athena for her creation of the olive. The daughters of Cecrops were the nurses of Erichthonius, another serpent-man who was in a sense the son of Athena. For he was born from the Earth when Hephaestus tried to rape Athena. Athena put the baby into a chest, and gave it to the three daughters of Cecrops forbidding them to open it. Two of them did so, were driven mad by the sight of a serpent in the chest, and hurled themselves down from the Acropolis. The idea that the virgin goddess Athena should bear a child was repugnant to the developed theology of the Greeks. The story is essentially that of the nurses of Dionysus, though the Athenian myth comes close to the original state of affairs in which the divine child was born of the goddess without a father.

Left. The temple of Poseidon on the south-east tip of Attica, a sea mark for any ship sailing by the Cyclades, seems to have been designed by the architect who built the temple of Hephaestus. All these temples formed part of Pericles' plan to mark out Athens as the centre of the league of island states. This view shows five of the nine restored columns of the southern side of the temple, which have been set up on a modern artificial base and look west along the southern coast of Attica and across the Saronic Gulf in the direction of Aegina.

Opposite above. The Acropolis at Athens. Greece consists of a series of small plains, many of them on the sea, surrounded by mountains. For protection from pirates, Greek cities were founded around easily defensible outcrops of limestone. Later, such a hill was called an acropolis. That of Athens is the most famous, and in the fifth century Pericles turned it into the sacred centre of Athens. On the left, to the west, is the formal entrance, the Propylaea, in the centre the Parthenon and between them the Erechtheum.

Opposite below. The Erechtheum, as it was called by the Greek traveller Pausanias in the second century A.D., is the most recent building on the Acropolis in Athens, constructed during the Peloponnesian war from about 420 B.C. But its site was the most sacred and oldest on the Acropolis, where a number of very ancient cults were sited, and this accounts for its odd shape.
To the left, facing north, a normal temple façade led into the ancient shrine of Poseidon and Erechtheus, also entered from the door to be seen by the sacred olive of Athena, and from stairs leading from the porch of the maidens. Here were the marks of Poseidon's trident, and the 'sea' or brackish pool which he created there. Here the cleft of the oracular hero Erechtheus, struck by lightning, was left open to the heaven and protected from flooding by the porch of the maidens. Outside, next to the olive, was the tomb of the serpent man Cecrops. Two other heroes also had shrines in the temple further east. Then came a wall, completely cutting off a temple of Athena, where the ancient wooden image of the goddess was kept, perhaps removed there from the older temple which the Parthenon had succeeded in all but sanctity. This temple was entered at a different level from a normal façade, which was balanced on the west by the false façade which can be seen above the door by the olive. The olive itself stood in a shrine of one of the daughters of Cecrops, who may also be symbolised in the Caryatids of the porch.

Tereus and Procne

The Athenian king lists contained a number of names which were brought into arbitrary genealogical relation to each other. One of them is Pandion, to whom is attached a fable about the hoopoe, the nightingale and the swallow, which explains their songs in terms of a fate which is made up of some of the elements of a supplanter myth. Procne and Philomela were sisters, daughters of Pandion, who married Procne to Tereus, king of Thrace. Tereus begot on her a son, Itys, but then raped her sister Philomela and cut out her tongue to prevent her telling what had happened. But she wove the story into a tapestry, and in this way told Procne, who took her revenge by serving up Itys as a meal for his father. Tereus pursued them with an axe, and the gods turned them into birds. Procne is the nightingale, who calls alternately upon Tereus and Itys,

Philomela (lover of song) is the swallow, who twitters unintelligibly, trying to tell her fate. Ovid reversed the names (and has been generally followed since). Tereus is the hoopoe, who pursues them crying 'Pou pou pou', 'Where, where, where?'

Another king is Erechtheus. The daughters of Erechtheus met fates which seem to be versions of those of the daughters of Cecrops. Orithyia was carried off by the North Wind, who helped the Athenians by destroying the ships of their enemies and begot on her Zetes and Calais, who were Argonauts. She was said to have been carried off from the banks of the Ilissus while gathering flowers, like Persephone: it would be appropriate if she had cast herself down from the Acropolis into the arms of her lover. The other daughters sacrificed themselves to ensure victory for their father in a war with Eleusis.

Theseus

Aegeus was the putative father of Theseus, the great Athenian hero. Perhaps because of his name, which could mean 'Founder', Theseus was honoured as the man responsible for the creation of the city-state of Athens by persuading all the local rulers to come and live in Athens and accept him as their overlord. As Heracles was taken over, especially by the Spartans, as the Dorian hero, so Theseus was built up as his Ionian counterpart. Heracles was made to found the Olympic games to commemorate one of his exploits, since athletic contests were the chief cultural activity of the Dorian aristocracy. The Athenians were never distinguished in these; but in everything else Theseus appears as either the companion or the imitator of Heracles.

But the Cretan connection shows that Theseus is more than a fictional hero representing Athenian aspirations, and it must constitute the oldest part of the myth. It starts before his birth in the reign of Aegeus, who had no son. The Delphic oracle told Aegeus not to loose the wine-skin before he got home. Not understanding this, he visited Pittheus at Troezen on his way back, who made him drunk and loosed on him his daughter Aethra. Laius too is said to have begotten Oedipus when drunk. Like him, Aegeus was begetting his supplanter and the wine-skin may reflect an orgiastic ritual as well as symbolising sexual intercourse.

In some of the stories concerning Theseus his father is Poseidon, who in late sources is explicitly stated to have lain with Aethra the same night. Theseus' father left his sword under a rock as a token of his paternity, as Poseidon did when he lay with Medusa the Gorgon and begot Chrysaor.

But there is no trace of a mortal twin. That a man's wife should bear a son to the god is, of course, one way in which succession in the female line can be reconciled with a patriarchal system.

Crete

Aegeus then returned to Athens, and it is here that the Cretan connection first appears in the person of Androgeus, son of Minos. Minos may have really been the title of the divine king of Crete and not a name. But all the stories are told of one man, the son of Zeus and Europa, who survived to the generation before the Trojan war. He had a brother, perhaps a twin, Rhadamanthys, whose name is definitely pre-Greek. He went into exile, ending with Minos as a judge in Hades, married to Alcmena. At first they merely judged between the dead, continuing the activity for which they were famous in life, perhaps an aspect of Minoan culture that had impressed the Greeks.

Bulls feature in the story of Minos. He got title to the kingdom when Poseidon sent a bull from the sea answering his prayer. For his failure to sacrifice it he suffered many evils. First was an unpleasant affliction that made it impossible for him to beget children: for he emitted not semen but snakes, scorpions and millipedes, which killed any woman. He was cured by Procris, the wife of Cephalus, who made an artificial woman which drew off all the animals, after which he was able to beget children normally. The legends of Crete are full of mechanical marvels like this. Another of them was Talos, the burning brazen man who patrolled Crete. Medea killed him, when the Argonauts passed, opening

Wall painting of Theseus leaving Ariadne on Naxos. Roman wall painting follows Hellenistic models no less than Roman mosaic, and mythological erotic panels such as this example from Herculaneum, overwhelmed in the eruption of A.D. 79, are common in both media. Ariadne awakes on the island of Naxos to find that Theseus had deserted her. British Museum, London.

the vein in his leg and letting out his magic blood.

In return, Procris got the wonderful dog that Cephalus took to Thebes, where it caught the monstrous vixen, together with a spear that never missed its mark. But it caused her death. For when Dawn carried off Cephalus, he pined for his wife, and Dawn sent him back disguised to see if Procris was faithful. He was able to seduce her, and she went to Crete, but when she came back played a similar trick, disguising herself as a boy and giving both hound and spear to Cephalus for a promise of his favours. Though they were reconciled, Procris secretly followed her husband as he went hunting each morning, and Dawn took her revenge by causing him to cast the spear at what he took to be a deer but was in fact his wife Procris.

The cured Minos begat sons and daughters on his wife Pasiphae, daughter of the Sun and sister of Aeetes king of Colchis. But she fell in love with the bull that should have been sacrificed. Daedalus, who had left Athens for killing an apprentice who had surpassed him, made her an artificial cow inside which she gratified her passion and conceived the Minotaur. This story, containing another Cretan mechanical marvel, is really an example that exhibits confusion of the three strata, god, king and sacred beast: the king perhaps impersonated the animal who represented the god in a sacred marriage. Daedalus also designed the labyrinth, named after the Cretan double axe, in which to keep the Minotaur. It is perhaps rather a ritual maze than a folk-memory of the Palace of Cnossus.

Minoan sea power is reflected in the story of Minos' son Catreus. His son Althaemenes went to Rhodes to avoid becoming his father's murderer: of course he failed, killing Catreus 'by accident' when he visited Rhodes. He also kicked his sister to death when she was raped by Hermes, who only caught her by spreading fresh bull hides in her path to make her slip. This must reflect a Rhodian ritual. Another of Minos' sons, Glaucus, was drowned in a jar of honey (there are Minoan burials, possibly in honey in great jars). A prophet, Polyidus, found the body after correctly describing the colour of a marvellous cow as a test, and was asked to revive it, which he did when he saw a snake bring the Herb of Life to the body of its dead mate. A Cretan ritual from the story of the supplanter seems to lie behind this tale.

Minos' third son Androgeus died at the horns of a bull. After triumphing at the Panathenaic festival, he was sent against the bull of Marathon, identified with the Bull from the Sea, which Heracles had taken from Crete and turned loose in Attica after showing it to Eurystheus. The news of his death was used to account for a ritual on the island of Paros, where they sacrificed to the Graces without garlands or flutes. It was said that Minos had started to sacrifice there, and in his grief at the news tore off his garland and stopped the flutes.

Minos later made war on Athens. First he captured Megara through the treachery of the king's daughter Scylla. For love of Minos she pulled out the hair that was her father's external soul. But Minos drowned her, tying her feet to a ship's stern, perhaps a ritual death. Like a goddess, she turned into a sea bird. Not even the sacrifice of three sisters (they were not the king's daughters, though probably victims of the same ritual as the daughters of Cecrops) could save the Athenians from Minos' fleet, and they were forced to agree to supply seven youths and maidens a year to be thrown to the Minotaur: there was a somewhat similar ritual at Corinth. This was the tribute that Theseus

joined. He slew the Minotaur, and by this exploit won the king's daughter, who betrayed her father and helped him.

The Exploits of Theseus

For when he was full grown Theseus recovered the sword from under the stone where his father had left it, and set out for Athens by the coast road along the Isthmus. On the way he dealt with six robbers and monsters which plagued the road, thus conveniently performing half the number of labours required to equal those of Heracles. The other six seem to be the Bull of Marathon, which Theseus disposed of finally when he got to Athens as his first exploit, the Minotaur, the Amazons, the Centaurs, the rape of Helen and the descent into Hades. In these last three he is associated with Pirithous, king of the Lapiths.

There are elements of folk tale in the stories of the robbers, some of whom may be decayed giants. Periphetes had an iron club which Theseus took over in imitation of Heracles. Sinis killed his victims by means of pine trees, probably by tearing them apart between two of the trees. The Athenians claimed that Theseus had founded the Isthmian Games in honour or expiation of Sinis. Sciron kicked men over the cliff to a man-eating turtle below: he suffered the same sacrificial fate himself and the turtle was turned to a rock.

Polypemon Procrustes hammered men into shape to fit his bed: Theseus was the man who fitted it exactly and turned the tables on Procrustes. Cercyon was a wrestler whom Theseus lifted up into the air, perhaps because like Antaeus he gained strength from the earth. The Crommyonian sow, called Phaea, 'grey', looks like a duplicate of Heracles' Erymanthian boar, and sometimes appears masculine in vase paintings. But all the rest reflect Athenian claims to the area, and the restoration of law and order is an appropriate activity for Theseus the political hero.

Theseus then successfully performed one exploit. He killed the Bull of Marathon which Heracles had set free. But his chief exploit was killing

Opposite top. Reverse of stater from Cnossus, 350–325 B.C. Cnossus, site of the palace of Minos, adopted as its symbol the labyrinth, a ritual maze with one path to the centre which leads right round the whole pattern. Such mazes are known from all over Europe and have been found engraved on megalithic monuments. They may be diagrams of a ritual dance. On either side are an arrowhead and a thunderbolt, both probably emblems of Zeus. British Museum, London.

Opposite centre. Bull-leaping, which may have left some trace in Greek mythology in the story of Theseus and the Minotaur. This is the only statuette, and the only representation which shows the feet of the leaper on the back of the bull – a posture which may, however, owe more to the technical requirements of bronze working than to reality. None of the other representations, Minoan as this and Mycenaean, on frescoes, vases and seals, are incompatible with tossing and goring, and none unquestionably show an acrobatic manoeuvre. It seems likely that 'bull-leaping' is a modern myth, and that the conscious or unconscious intention of the encounters between man and bull was the death by goring of the former. It is always dangerous to make inferences about beliefs and practices from artistic representations (which may show not what happened but what was supposed to happen) in the absence of literary evidence. British Museum, London.

Opposite bottom. Theseus killing the Minotaur. The decoration of an Attic wine cup became more difficult as the stem got longer and the cup shallower. From 550 B.C. the band between the handles was decorated with a frieze of miniature figures, as in the vase signed by the potter Glaucytes. Both sides of the vase show great exploits: on one the Calydonian Boar hunt (page 70); on the other Theseus killing the Minotaur. Theseus wears an animal skin like Heracles, the great monster slayer, and the exploit is watched by Ariadne on the right and Athena on the left. Behind each of them is a procession of alternate women and men. Staatliche Antikansammlungen und Glyptothek, Munich.

Left. Lapith and Centaur. The metopes on the south side of the Parthenon all had a single theme, the battle of the Lapiths and Centaurs. The figures have the sad repose of developed classical art. The Centaur has nothing bestial about him, but is the ideal type of an older man, as the Lapith is of a young man. Elgin Marbles, British Museum, London.

the Minotaur, in which he was helped by Minos' daughter Ariadne. She gave him the ball of thread that would enable him to return successfully from the centre of the ritual Labyrinth after killing the Minotaur with his bare hands. Afterwards he left Ariadne, asleep on Naxos. She was soon consoled by Dionysus. In the local ritual of Dionysus she was his consort.

A variant of the exploit, appropriate for a son of Poseidon, may appear in the story of the contest between Theseus and Minos on the voyage to Crete. Zeus thundered in a clear sky to attest his fatherhood of Minos. Theseus by his father's aid recovered a golden ring that Minos threw into the sea, and a golden crown as well. But whatever form the exploit took, it ended predictably in the 'accidental' death of Aegeus. Theseus 'forgot' to change the sails to the colour that would announce success, and Aegeus threw himself down from the point on the Acropolis from which the sea can be seen. His death is clearly related to the similar fates of kings' daughters at Athens.

Minos shut up Daedalus in the Labyrinth of which he had given the secret to Ariadne. But he and his son Icarus escaped on wings (another Cretan invention). Icarus emulated Phaethon and went too near the sun. The wax of his wings melted and he was precipitated into the sea. Minos pursued Daedalus to Sicily, where he discovered him by a typical piece of Daedalic technology, a shell threaded with the help of an ant. But the local king's daughters saved Daedalus by boiling Minos immortal after his bath, like the the daughters of Pelias.

Theseus and Hippolytus

The rest of Theseus' life is anti-climax. He went with Heracles against the Amazons, and carried off the queen as his bride, defeating the Amazon invasion of Athens that he had thus provoked. Theseus' son Hippolytus, was named after his mother, the Amazon queen, and it seems just possible that the Amazon legend was originally Athenian and not part of the story of Heracles. Then Theseus joined Pirithous in the war of the Lapiths and the Centaurs, which, like the war of the gods and the Giants, was used in the fifth century to symbolise the triumph of Athenian civilisation over the barbarian.

Also with Pirithous he carried out his last two exploits, both of which suggest elements of a sacred marriage. For both Theseus and Pirithous determined to marry daughters of Zeus. Theseus chose Helen (the genealogists calculated that she was then only ten or twelve). Then he went with Pirithous down to Hades to get Persephone for him — that is, the Girl who is brought back in the spring. But

Above. Theseus carrying off Helen. Pirithous draws his sword to ward off opposition as Helen's servant vainly tries to save her. Staatliche Antikensammlungen und Glyptothek, Munich.

Above left. Theseus and the Minotaur. This vase of about 550 B.C. shows a robust Theseus killing a subdued Minotaur with his sword in the vulnerable part of the neck where the helmet joined the breastplate in an armoured hoplite. The six Attic youths, one with a fillet in his hand, three of the others with wreaths, stand on either side of him, and he has put his cloak down on a rock. Ashmolean Museum, Oxford.

Opposite. A silver relief found at Perugia, which formed part of the decoration of a chariot ornamented with plaques of bronze and silver. It was made in Ionia, possibly at Clazomenae, in the sixth century, and its journey illustrates the extent of Greek contacts with Etruria, and their ability to manufacture for a market, since it is perhaps unlikely that the chariot was exported as well. The Amazons (if they are indeed female since the hair is little longer and the bust no more developed than that of many undoubtedly male statues) on their rearing horses are an appropriate decoration for a war chariot. The right-hand warrior appears to be spearing the fallen figure on the ground, which is also being trodden by the horses. British Museum, London.

Persephone, the death goddess, held them fast on magic thrones of rock, to which they stuck, so that they could not move, like Hera on the magic throne that Hephaestus made. While they were there, Castor and Pollux, the brothers of Helen, took her back to Sparta. Theseus was rescued by Heracles, who came down to fetch Cerberus, and whose great strength tore him away, though he left a portion of himself behind, bequeathing to all subsequent Athenians thin buttocks.

Theseus returned to find a member of the house of Erechtheus on the throne, Menestheus, whom Castor and Pollux had restored from exile. Theseus fled to the island of Scyros, where the king gave him the traditional death of an Athenian king by hurling him down from a height.

But before he left Athens, Theseus had been responsible for the death of his son Hippolytus in circumstances which suggest his sacrifice as a surrogate, but which could have led to Theseus' own death. Theseus' wife Phaedra, the sister of Ariadne, fell in love with Hippolytus, and her nurse tried to procure him for her.

But Hippolytus, like Bellerophon and later Peleus, played the virtuous Joseph. Ashamed, Phaedra hanged herself, preserving her good name with a letter accusing Hippolytus. Theseus at once accused his son of trying to supplant him. The nurse had bound Hippolytus with an oath, and he was unable to rebut the accusations. Whereupon Theseus invoked one of the curses given by his father Poseidon, and another Bull from the Sea came to cause Hippolytus' death in a manner appropriate to his name 'Horse loosed'. His frightened team bolted with him as he drove into exile

along the coast road which Theseus had himself taken to Athens, and he was dragged to death over the rocks. Finally the virgin goddess Artemis appeared to reconcile father and son, and to institute the cult of her favourite Hippolytus. But behind the chaste figures of goddess and devoté it is possible to discern the consort of a crueller goddess, who regularly chooses the man who shall supplant him, slaying him after or during the course of a ritual chariot race.

Birth of Erichthonius. Gaia, 'Earth', hands a baby to Athena while Nike, 'Victory', holds out the swaddling band. Zeus holding a stylised thunderbolt looks on, supported by a girl over whose head is written 'Oinanthe is beautiful'. She is probably one of the daughters of Cecrops, who took over the infant Erichthonius. The scene shows that Erichthonius was originally the son of the mother-goddess, a role Athena lost at Athens, where she remained 'nurse of youths'. British Museum, London.

The Trojan War

The last great communal enterprise of the Greek heroes was the Sack of Troy. Though it succeeded in its aim, the difficulties were great, and an air of failure and defeat hangs over it all. Few of the heroes returned to find their kingdoms secure, and few of the dynasties survived for more than a few generations. For this there is a historical reason. Many of the leaders came from new families with much shorter genealogies than those of the children of Cadmus, of Aeolus and of Danaus. Greece had presumably already been unsettled by further migrations, and the new situation may be reflected in the rise of Mycenae rather than Thebes as the dominant power in Greece. Mycenaean settlements have been found all over the eastern Mediterranean, on the coast of Asia Minor, in Cyprus and in Syria. It is likely that Mycenaean Greeks controlled Crete during the last great period of the Palace at Cnossus. Something of this may lie behind the myth of Theseus and the Minotaur, just as the sack of Troy may reflect an episode in the period of the expansion. But myth and epic are not history.

The great leader of the Greek expedition is Agamemnon, king of Mycenae. His place in a list of what seem to be shepherd kings, deriving their authority from Hermes, the god of flocks, is given very early in the *Iliad*. Hephaestus made the sceptre, and gave it to Zeus who passed it on to Hermes. From there it went first to Pelops, striker of horses, then to Atreus, shepherd of hosts, and on his death to his brother Thyestes, of many lambs, and last of all to Agamemnon. This is not the same as the genealogy, which begins with Pelops' father Tantalus in Lydia.

Tantalus

Tantalus is one of those divine kings admitted to the table of Zeus and eventually punished for some act of presumption, like Ixion and perhaps Bellerophon. He is the son of Zeus, though there were some attempts to link him with Thebes, where his daughter Niobe seems to have belonged. There are various accounts of his sin, that he revealed the counsels of the gods or stole ambrosia to give to men: but they all add up to the ritual that made the king's son immortal as the king's surrogate.

In a variant Tantalus, like a Titan, is buried under Mount Sipylus, for perjury, or perhaps abuse of his oath, like Sisyphus. The story concerns the theft of a golden dog from the shrine of Zeus in Crete by Pandareus, who entrusted it to Tantalus. But when he asked for it back, Tantalus swore some oath to Zeus which denied all knowledge of it. Pandareus, to whom Demeter had granted the ability to eat anything without suffering for it, may have been involved in the punishment, for his daughters were orphaned and brought up by the goddesses. One married at Thebes, like Niobe, and became the Theban Procne. The others were carried off by the Harpies to serve the Furies. Too much of their story is missing for it to be possible to explain its basis.

Tantalus' final crime was to ask the gods to a banquet, at which, wishing like Lycaon to test them, he served them up his own son Pelops boiled in a cauldron. All the gods but Demeter, who was grieving for her daughter, abstained from the horrid and impious meal, which was, of course, originally the reverse, holy and a duty. Tantalus was punished in Hades by being placed thirsty in a pool of water which drained away when he tried to drink it, just as the fruits above his head were snatched away as he reached for them.

Pelops, Atreus and Thyestes

Pelops, however, was rejuvenated in the cauldron, and got an ivory shoulder to replace the one that had been gnawed. Poseidon gave him a winged chariot, to enable Pelops to beat Oenomaus, another son of Ares, in the chariot race for the hand of his daughter Hippodameia. But Hippodameia bribed Myrtilus, a son of Hermes, to replace with wax the pins that held on the wheels of her father's chariot. The wax sheared on the bend and Oenomaus was killed in a race that was certainly 'fixed' to allow the supplanter to win. Thus Pelops became king of Elis.

Myrtilus is a complicating factor, who may belong to another version perhaps implied in the tradition of the sceptre. For he tried to rape Hippodameia (perhaps claiming his reward) and Pelops killed him. But he may be the father of Thyestes, one of the two, and perhaps twin, sons of Pelops. The other was Atreus, but there was a third, Chrysippus, a nymph's son, whom Pelops loved the best, and whom the other two killed. They were driven into exile but returned after Pelops' death to rule the kingdom. This is clearly the sacrifice of a son, perhaps in a form that enables the father's true sons to inherit from him, unless Atreus and Thyestes were originally not sons but supplanters.

They alternated in ruling the kingdom by a series of tricks on one another. The symbol of sovereignty, as at Orchomenus, was a golden lamb, which Zeus caused to appear in the flocks of Atreus. But his wife stole it and gave it to her lover Thyestes. Atreus came back when Zeus made the sun go backwards and set in the east (this ought to mean 'never') and served up Thyestes' own children to him, boiled in a cauldron. Possibly the return of Atreus is designed to remove from Thyestes the guilt of having sacrificed his children, as the ritual of his house obliged him to do. But the blood guilt is perpetrated.

Thyestes was revenged by his daughter's son, who was suckled by a goat sent by Hermes and was called Aegisthus. He was therefore perhaps originally Hermes' son. But in the tragic version which survives the father is Thyestes, but the child is reared by Atreus. He eventually killed Atreus at a sacrifice after having been sent to kill Thyestes, whom Atreus held in prison. But Thyestes recognised the sword which he had left as a token when begetting Aegisthus. The motifs of incest and parricide point certainly to a fifth-century tragedy, the plot of which is based on a number of mythical elements. But the purpose of the alternating kingship is clear: to protect the inheritance and also to shift the responsibility for the sacrifices.

Atreus' two (or twin) sons, Agamemnon and Menelaus, fled to Aetolia. They returned with Tyndareus, who had married the king's daughter, when Heracles restored him to Sparta. Tyndareus was driven out by his brother and won Leda as his bride in Aetolia. Heracles was involved because Tyndareus' brother joined the other side in Heracles' war at Pylos. Some historical truth may lie behind these tangled tales of sacking and explusions.

Leda

Leda and her children are connected not only with the Trojan war but also with the Calydonian myths. Her father was the brother and perhaps the twin of Evenus, son of Ares, and her sons Castor and Pollux fought with Idas, who won Evenus' daughter, and his twin Lynceus. But Zeus

loved Leda, and came to her in the form of a swan. Quite exceptionally, she is said to have borne two sets of twins, one of each pair being mortal and one immortal: one pair was female, Helen and Clytemnestra, the only set of female twins in Greek mythology. Even more exceptionally, Leda is said to have laid either one or two eggs.

The quarrel of Castor and Pollux with Idas and Lynceus arose when they carried off the daughter of Leucippus, 'White Horse', who had been promised to the other pair. Another version makes them quarrel over the division of the spoils of a cattle raid, and contains folk-tale elements making use of the special talents of Idas, who could eat anything at high speed,

and Lynceus, who was keen-sighted. Idas cut one of the cows into four parts, and proposed that half the booty go to the man who finished his portion first, and half to the second. Then he gobbled up his and his brother's before the Dioscuri even started. So they laid an ambush for Idas and Lynceus, but the latter's keen sight discovered it. Both mortal twins were killed. But Zeus struck Idas with lightning, which should mean he received cult as a hero in Hades, and carried Pollux up to heaven. But for

love of his brother he spent one day with him in Hades, and the next took him up into heaven with him. This accounts for the two kinds of cult received by the Dioscuri.

All the heroes of Greece came to woo Helen, but the contest, if there ever was one, has been suppressed. Instead there is another folk tale, of the suitors' oath, which is used to account for the expedition of all the Greeks against Troy. Tyndareus feared to favour one suitor over another, until Odysseus advised him to make them all swear loyalty to the chosen one. This was Menelaus, whose brother, Agamemnon, was already married to Clytemnestra, Helen's mortal twin. Both the sons of Atreus, therefore, owed their kingdoms to their wives.

Achilles

Though the Trojan war was triggered off by the rape of Helen, its origins lay further back in the house of Achilles, the greatest of the Greek heroes at Troy. In the *Iliad* he is often called Aeacides, not son but grandson of Aeacus, who was the most just of all the Greeks and ended up in Hades as the third judge with Minos and Rhadamanthys. His reputation for

justice seems to rest on his fame as a rain-maker. Greece was afflicted by a drought attributed to the impious deed of Pelops, who murdered an Arcadian king and scattered his limbs over the land. Aeacus then ascended the mount of all the Greeks on Aegina, and prayed successfully to his father Zeus for rain. Traces of the ritual survive in the story of his children.

His mother was the nymph Aegina, and his people, the Myrmidons, were ants whom Zeus turned into men, in a variant of the myth of Deucalion and Pyrrha, when Aeacus was alone on the island. Aeacus had two sons, Peleus and Phocus: a third, Telamon, is really a local hero of Salamis, if he is not simply the belt which supports the shield-hero Ajax. The mother of Phocus, and originally perhaps of Peleus as well, was a seal-maiden; sea nymphs recur in the family history. The two sons quarrelled (one should be the son of a god) and Peleus killed Phocus 'accidentally' by a cast of the discus: there are a number of familiar ritual motifs here.

Peleus went into exile and appeared as a potential supplanter in two places. First in Phthia, where he married the king's daughter, he 'acciden-

tally' killed his host with his spear at the Calydonian Boar hunt. Then at Iolcus, where he wrestled with Atalanta at the funeral games of Pelias (which looks like an exploit), he played the virtuous Joseph with his host's wife. His host could not kill Peleus, but took him hunting on Mount Pelion and stole away his ash spear, which was probably magic, and which none but him could wield. Peleus escaped from the beasts up a tree, from which he was rather tamely rescued by Chiron the good centaur, who had originally given him the spear.

Above. Peleus treed by a lion and a boar. Greek black-figure vases were sometimes drawn on a white ground which covered the red clay, as in a wine jug of the late sixth century by the painter of London. It shows Peleus taking refuge in a tree from the attack of a lion and a boar after his host Acastus had robbed him of his magic spear. Acastus' wife had tried to seduce Peleus and, failing, accused him to her husband. But lion and boar recur as sacred animals in many exploits, and the vase, as often happens, suggests an earlier ritual in which Peleus was the supplanter who killed Acastus. Metropolitan Museum of Art, New York. Purchase: 1946, Joseph Pulitzer Bequest.

Left. Marble statue of Athena. The pediments of the temple of Aphaea on Aegina both show Athena presiding over scenes of battle, perhaps between Greeks and Trojans (for there is an archer in one scene), symbolising the victory over the Persians in which the Aeginetans joined with the Athenians. Aphaea was identified with Britomartis, one of the forms of the Artemis worshipped in Crete. But the temple suggests she may also have had qualities that could lead to her identification with Athena. The statue of about 480 B.C. from the pediment was originally painted and decorated with bronze or gold for which the holes can be seen. The breast of the goddess probably bore the gorgon head and her right hand held a spear. Staatliche Antikensammlungen und Glyptothek, Munich.

The original ending of the tale may have been suppressed and have contained a contest. Acastus stole Peleus' share of the spoils of the hunt, but Peleus proved his title to them by producing the tongues which he had cut out, a common folk-tale motif.

As a reward for his chastity the gods gave Peleus the hand of Thetis, for whom Zeus and Poseidon had contended, but both abandoned her when they learnt that her son was to be mightier than his father. As always where Thetis is concerned, this is a watered down version of the succession myth. In other versions Thetis is a typical water nymph, who is captured by the hero and held through her various transformations. After this he might keep her as his wife provided she never spoke to him.

The gods came to the wedding of Peleus and Thetis, but Strife, presumably because she was not invited (another folk-tale motif), cast among them a golden apple inscribed 'for the fairest', the contest for which occasioned the Trojan war. The surviving child of the marriage was Achilles.

Thetis had destroyed six previous children by putting them on the fire or boiling them in a cauldron to make them immortal. When she was doing the same to Achilles Peleus interrupted her, and she spoke to him and had to return to the sea. She had made him immortal and invulnerable except for the heel, which Peleus supplied like Pelops' shoulder blade, but from the bone of a swift-footed giant. The version that Achilles was dipped in the water of the Styx is much later.

Trojan Stories

Troy, the modern Hissarlik, was a fortified palace site from the beginning of the Bronze Age. It had cultural links with Greece from the time of the first Greek speakers about 1900 B.C., who may have entered Greece from Asia Minor through Troy. So it is not surprising that the genealogical list of Trojan kings is as long as that of the Thebans, or that the mythical history of Troy is interwoven with that of Greece. Indeed, the first king, Dardanus, is said to have been a brother of the culture

hero Iasion, a consort of Demeter. In one version Iasion was struck by lightning for his presumption, and Dardanus, like his brother a son of Zeus, floated across to Asia on a raft of inflated hides. There were no ships until Danaus invented them to escape with his daughters from Egypt.

Much of the early genealogy is artificial, though already known to the *Iliad*. Dardanus and his grandson, Tros, are derived from the names Dardanians and Trojans used in the *Iliad*. His great-grandson Ilus is derived from the city of Ilium, the site of which, like Thebes, was indicated by a cow. The name of his son, Erichthonius, is more appropriate to an earthborn king. Erichthonius was very rich, as befits a son of earth, not in cattle but in horses. He was said to have had three thousand mares at pasture in the marshes of the river Scamander. The best of the colts were sired by the North wind, and were so fast that they did not bend the ears of corn when they ran over them. It is possible that Poseidon also had a hand in this horse-breeding, which reflects the historical fact that the plain of Troy was one of the places where it was possible to pasture horses in large numbers. Zeus gave mares, the best in the east, as the price of Ganymede, son of Tros and brother of Ilus, when he carried him off to heaven to be his cupbearer. But the story was probably first that of the sacifice of a son.

Laomedon, the son of Ilus, promised those mares to Heracles, who touched at Troy when returning with the girdle of the Amazon Hippolyte, and saved Hesione, Laomedon's daughter, from a sea monster to which she was exposed. But he was cheated of his reward. The story, modelled on that of Perseus and Andromeda, may in fact have been borrowed to motivate Heracles' second visit to Troy when he sacked the city. But Laomedon had a reputation as a cheat. He also cheated Apollo and Poseidon of their wages when they had to serve him for a year as punishment for the conspiracy from which Thetis saved Zeus. Apollo herded Laomedon's cows, as he had done those of Admetus, while Poseidon built an impregnable wall round Troy. Laomedon not only refused to pay them their agreed wages, but threatened to sell them into slavery with their ears cut off to mark their status. It was in revenge for this treatment that Poseidon sent the sea-monster to Troy.

Heracles returned to sack Troy in what may be a piece of genuine saga, evidence for continuous hostility between Greece and Troy. He took with him Telamon, who was the first to breach the wall because he knew the one piece of it that had been built not by Poseidon but by his father Aeacus. Heracles would have slain him for this presumption, but he averted his fate by the timely dedication of an altar to Heracles the Glorious Victor. In gratitude, Heracles assigned him Laomedon's daughter Hesione, who should have been Heracles' reward on

his previous visit, if the pattern of the supplanter were followed. When she was allowed to ransom one of the captives, she chose her brother. Telamon's bastard son by Hesione is more Trojan than Greek. Though he fought for the Greeks at Troy he used the eastern bow, and ended up in Cyprus. His name Teucer is that of a Trojan king, and may be that of an eastern god.

Priam's brother Tithonus was one of the consorts of Dawn, like Orion and Cephalus: indeed he was sometimes said to be the son of Cephalus. She begged for him the gift of immortality, but the jealous gods granted only the letter of her prayer, withholding eternal youth, as they did from the Sibyl. So Tithonus withered away and Dawn shut him up in his chamber, where little more than a disembodied voice, he may have turned into a grasshopper.

Above. Erotic scenes, heterosexual or homosexual, are appropriate to the inside of a drinking cup used at male drinking parties, where the only women present were non-Athenian courtesans or slave entertainers. The abduction of Ganymede by Zeus – a myth perhaps first used by Pindar as a kind of perverse charter myth authorising such conduct – is here assimilated in a fine composition by the Penthesilea painter of about 460-450 B.C., to the pursuit of a young love, deemed to have given his consent by accepting the love-gift of a fighting cock, but now reluctant, by an older, bearded man, safely identified as Zeus by a formalised winged thunderbolt on the left. Museo Nazionale Archeologico, Ferrara.

Opposite. Peleus wrestling with Thetis was a favourite subject of Greek vase painters, and from imported vases it was copied by the engravers of Etruscan mirror-backs, for which it formed a suitably erotic subject. As time went by these engravings became increasingly Etruscan in style, as is that shown which dates from perhaps the fourth rather than the fifth century. Thetis is beginning to be assimilated to the style of a winged Etruscan female demon. Peleus is a boy and not a man. British Museum, London.

A similar consort may be seen in Anchises, a descendant of Assaracus, brother of Ilus and Ganymede. The goddess Aphrodite actually bore him a son, Aeneas, the only son of an Olympian goddess by a mortal known to Greek mythology. Aeneas was important to later genealogies. The story of his rescue of his father from Troy appears early. But in the *Hymn* to Aphrodite, Anchises knows that the consorts of goddesses do not have a flourishing life, and Aphrodite warns him that if he discloses the maternity of his son he will be struck by lightning. It is a reasonable inference that Anchises too ended up as the object of cult, and the desire among those who claimed descent from Aeneas to continue this cult may be the explanation of the stories of the rescue of Anchises. The family also claimed the divine Trojan mares, saying that Anchises had stolen them from Laomedon.

The Trojan royal house has much closer and more frequent dealings with the gods than any Greek family. This relationship continues in the time of Priam, whose daughter Cassandra is a 'bride of Apollo', and inspired prophetess. But because she refused the god her favours he spat in her mouth, that nobody might believe her, and she could safely prophesy the doom of Troy without in any way altering the course of history.

The Judgement of Paris

There is a story about Priam's son Paris that suggests a supplanter. His mother Hecuba dreamed she bore a firebrand that destroyed the city, and the child was therefore exposed, only to be suckled by a bear and brought up by a shepherd. No god is associated with a bear, only Artemis, which suggests that Paris was once, like Aeneas, a goddess's son. It is therefore not surprising that the other three goddesses made him the judge when they strove for the golden apple inscribed 'for the fairest' that Strife cast among them at the wedding of Peleus and Thetis. Aphrodite offered Paris lust, and he praised her, rejecting the other goddesses, Hera and Athena, who offered him kingship

and victory in war respectively.

Behind the story, which is alluded to in the *Iliad* in the slightly contemptuous form given above (though only the gift of Aphrodite is mentioned), can be seen the son and consort of a mother-goddess, who has made him every woman's darling. His wife Helen seems once to have been a Spartan tree-goddess, and he went to Sparta to carry her off as if he were a supplanter.

Menelaus with Agamemnon gathered most of the heroes of Greece with only token ones of the Thebans and the Athenians. There was a persistent tradition that Troy was not taken until the twentieth year after the rape of Helen. The delay is accounted for in two ways. First, it took some time to persuade all the suitors to come on the expedition. Odysseus at least was reluctant. He had advised Tyndareus to exact the oath because he wanted to marry Penelope, daughter of Tyndareus' brother Icarius, who tried to persuade him to settle in Sparta. But Odysseus carried Penelope off in his chariot, followed by Icarius, who kept on begging her to stay but gave up when she veiled her face. Agamemnon went to Ithaca, off the west coast of Greece, to persuade Odysseus to join him.

Odysseus was reluctant to join the expedition and at one time was said to have feigned madness, yoking an ox and an ass to the plough and sowing his fields with salt. The stratagem was discovered when the Greeks put Telemachus in the path of the plough. This is a decayed version of the exploit of yoking beasts, and of the sacrifice of a son. Odysseus himself discovered Achilles, whom his mother had hidden among the women of Scyros, hoping in this way to save him from an early death.

The second reason for the delay in taking Troy was that the Greeks got lost and went to Mysia to the south of it. There Telephus the king repulsed them, until Dionysus tripped him with a vine branch and Achilles wounded him in the thigh. Telephus was Heracles' son and a typical supplanter, who was exposed and suckled by a doe, killed his mother's

Above. Ganymede and the eagle. Seals were used in the ancient world in most circumstances where nowadays a signature attests the genuineness of a letter or a money transaction. The gem engraver's work was therefore highly confidential, and his art was partly for this reason highly regarded in antiquity. Like all other Greek art forms, a high proportion of the subjects are taken from mythology. This garnet of the first century B.C. shows Ganymede and the eagle which, according to one version, carried him off to heaven. He is giving the eagle a drink from a cup, a clear reference to his task in heaven. But he sits on a rock under a tree, dressed as a shepherd in a Trojan cap, a type used also for Paris, and the scene is therefore on earth. It was only for the actual abduction that Zeus assumed the form of an eagle. Ionides Collection.

Opposite. The body of a terracotta statue of Zeus and Ganymede found in excavations since the Second World War fitted a head found at the end of the nineteenth century. It retains traces of the original colours. The black-bearded Zeus has a red cloak with black border. Ganymede carries the cock which Zeus has given him as a love gift. The whole stands over three feet high, and adorned the top of the pediment of a small temple or shrine. It was made by a Peloponnesian in Corinthian clay about 470 B.C. Archaeological Museum, Olympia.

uncles and came to Mysia, where he seems to be a figure in a fertility cult. For the wound would not heal until, like the magic impotence inflicted on his son by Phylacus when gelding rams, it was touched with the rust of the spear that made the wound. Telephus came to the Greek camp, and promised to navigate the Greeks to Troy in return.

Even so the Greek fleet was unable to leave Aulis in Boeotia, though an omen told them that Troy would fall in the tenth year. A snake devoured eight sparrows together with their mother, representing the nine full years they would consume at the siege, and then was turned to stone. The fleet was held by contrary winds until Agamemnon's daughter Iphigenia was sacrificed to Artemis. She was brought under the pretence that she was going to be married to Achilles.

Various not very convincing reasons are given why a sacrifice was required. One version linked the sacrifice with the ritual at Brauron, another with that of the Sacred Spring, when everything born in a year was vowed to the god. In fact, in Greek mythology and especially at Athens, daughters are often sacrificed for the victory of an army, or sacrifice themselves. This is just another case, softened by the story that a deer was substituted at the last moment by the goddess, who carried off Iphigenia to be her priestess among the Tauri of the Crimea, where human sacrifices could safely be attributed to barbarians.

The Greeks went first to Tenedos, where Achilles killed the king, a son of Apollo, thus ensuring his own early death. On Tenedos, Philoctetes was bitten by a snake and marooned on Lemnos because the Greeks could not bear the smell of the suppurating wound. The bow of Heracles, which Philoctetes had been given as a reward for igniting his pyre, was necessary to the capture of Troy, and this story conveniently gets it and him out of the way. When they finally reached

Opposite. The Judgement of Paris. The Penthesilea painter, working from 475 B.C., unlike some of his followers, could decorate a toilet box with an appropriate subject without descending into sentimentality. The Judgement of Paris, with the inscription twice repeated 'The boy is beautiful', runs right round the jar. Paris is seen sitting on a rock, wearing a travelling hat and carrying a club. Behind him is an older man with a thin stick. He may be only a spectator to fill the space, possibly Zeus or Priam. Hermes, bearded and similarly dressed as a traveller, but identified by his attributes, comes to fetch him to the goddesses, who face one another on the other side of the vase. Metropolitan Museum of Art, New York, Rogers Fund, 1907.

Above. The other side of the silver cup from Hoby. Odysseus, recognisable by his hat, is trying to persuade the injured Philoctetes, shown as a beggar with staff and bandaged foot but no bow, to return to Troy which could not be taken without him. Odysseus concealed his identity, and used the son of Achilles, Neoptolemus, to work on Philoctetes. When persuasion failed, Heracles resolved the resulting impasse by reminding Philoctetes that it was the will of the gods that Troy should fall and that he should contribute. Nationalmuseet, Copenhagen.

Left. Sacrifice of Iphigenia. This was a subject that appealed to dramatists throughout the fifth century. But both literature and art stressed the pathos of the scene and the grief of the father. This vase painting is quite calm and fully aware of the divine intentions for Iphigenia. The presence of Apollo, top left, balancing his sister Artemis with her bow and with the typical crossed bands of vases of this kind, may point to his instructions to Orestes to rescue his sister from the Crimea. As it is, Iphigenia seems almost to be turning into the deer which stands behind her rearing up on to the altar, and which is clearly the target of the sacrificial knife wielded by a man whose lack of distress identifies him as Calchas rather than Agamemnon. On the left an attendant holds the garlands for the victim and perhaps the flour that was sprinkled on it. British Museum, London.

Below. Achilles slaying a Trojan. Towards the end of the fourth century B.C. the native Etruscan style of vase painting introduced a new character into many scenes, a native demon. This does not represent a new development in Etruscan religion; rather, as long as the artists followed their Greek models strictly, there was no room for a demon in the pictures. Here Charon, the Greek name adopted from the boatman who ferried souls across the Styx to the underworld, stands by with his hammer as Achilles, mislabelled AIFAS, that is Ajax, kills one of the Trojan captives at the tomb of Patroclus with a downward stab into the jugular. Bibliothèque Nationale, Paris.

Opposite. Achilles and Penthesilea. Terracotta was the preferred material for sculptural details in early Greece because of its cheapness and the ease with which it could be modelled. It is virtually indestructible, though fragile, and is not liable, like stone, to reworking. Part of an early Attic relief, of about 600 B.C., decorated the tomb of a warrior, since it shows Achilles, the ideal warrior, victorious in a duel. He is shown facing left so that the gorgon head of his shield may be seen. Part of a dead warrior at his feet is labelled Aenea, so that his opponent must have been an Amazon, presumably Penthesilea, the queen who led the Amazons to Troy to help the Trojans. Metropolitan Museum of Art, New York. Samuel D. Lee Fund, 1942.

Below. Achilles sparing Priam. Some metal vessels have survived from ancient times by being buried for security in unsettled times and countries. A silver cup of the Roman period signed both in Greek and Latin by Cheirisophus (the name means 'Hand-wise') was found at Hoby in Denmark. One side shows the classic scene which ends the *Iliad*, and exploits its poignancy rhetorically. Priam kisses the hands that slew his son, and Achilles spares him, when he thinks of the aged father who would in his turn mourn the dead Achilles. Nationalmuseet, Copenhagen.

Troy, the Trojans refused to return Helen and broke the truce when Menelaus won the single combat with Paris that was supposed to settle the issue. Then the Greeks settled down to the long siege of Troy.

The Sack of Troy

The *Iliad* is a straightforward story of the fighting at Troy, told in personal terms. Achilles quarrels with Agamemnon because his honour is slighted when his prize, Briseis, is taken to replace Chryseis, whom Agamemnon is forced to return to her father. He withdraws to his tent, but allows his friend Patroclus to help the Greeks when Zeus permits the Trojans to reach the ships. He rejoins the fight for personal reasons when Patroclus is killed, and kills Hector as an act of personal revenge. He mistreats Hector's body, dragging it round Troy, but is finally moved to restore it to Priam, who reminds him of the father he will never see again. Various episodes from the Iliad can sometimes be explained in terms of myth and ritual – even perhaps the

chase of Hector round the walls of Troy, since Achilles is conventionally 'swift-footed' – but such explanations are irrelevant to the poem.

The myths of the Trojan war are outside the *Iliad*, and are often concerned with the conditions that had to be fulfilled before Troy could be taken. Thus the first man to land was fated to be killed. It was Protesilaus, who received cult at his tomb in Thrace opposite Troy; elms grew in the precinct, and their leaves faded when they could see Troy. Thus, too, Achilles ambushed the young Troilus and killed him. If Troilus reached twenty Troy was safe, so no doubt he was killed on the very eve of the fatal birthday. Odysseus and Diomede stole the horses of the Thracian Rhesus on the night he arrived at Troy: if they but drank the waters of Scamander Troy was safe. Rhesus sounds as though he may have been a 'son of Ares' once: he was probably the object of cult in an oracular cave.

As Patroclus died for killing Sarpedon, the son of Zeus, so Hector's death was avenged by that of Achilles. But before that, Achilles killed two of the exotic allies of the Trojans. The first was Memnon, son of the Dawn and Tithonus. He was buried on the Hellespont, and once a year birds went to sweep the grave and sprinkle it with water. There was evidently a tendency to assume that all the local cult-heroes had met their death at Troy. The 'birds' may have been women performing a bird dance. The other victim was Penthesilea, queen of the Amazons, who came to Troy to be purified for the 'accidental' murder of her sister Hippolyte, mother of Hippolytus. The pattern suggests that she may have been recruited as an ally by marrying one of

Opposite top. This fragment from 560–550 B.C. by Nearchos has often recalled the passage in the *Iliad* when Achilles' horses are suddenly able to answer his reproaches for deserting Patroclus by reminding him of his own rapidly approaching fate, which Achilles has long known and which makes his quest for glory the more urgent. But the horses' names are not the same, and in fact the vase showed Thetis and Hephaestus bringing Achilles his armour. National Museum, Athens.

Opposite centre. Suicide of Ajax. The Etruscan gem engravers seem to have taken their subjects from Greek vases, which were imported into Etruria in large quantities and later imitated there, rather than from Greek gems. But a fifth century example, of which the impression is shown, is very well adapted to its medium. The suicide of Ajax, when he was not awarded the arms of Achilles, was a subject whose cruelty particularly appealed to the Etruscans. Museum of Fine Arts, Boston, Massachusetts. Bartlett Fund.

Opposite bottom. Diomede with the Palladium. Because they were intended as seals, most Greek ringstones, like this fourth century chalcedony one, are engraved in intaglio to produce an effective relief impression. Diomede, who has just succeeded in stealing the Palladium or sacred image from the Temple of Athena in Troy, is stealthily tiptoeing with drawn sword to avoid discovery. The Palladium is shown as a tiny but perfect image. Such totems were really either meteoric stones fallen from heaven or a primitive and roughly shaped tree trunk containing the god whose presence made the city inviolable. Museum of Fine Arts, Boston, Massachusetts. Bartlett Fund.

Left. Suicide of Ajax. This bronze statuette from Etruria was attached to the rim of some bronze object, perhaps acting as one of the handles. Ajax's attitude suggests that he was appealing to somebody on the other side of the object, perhaps Athena, who had tried to save him from the consequence of his madness. Museo Archeologico, Florence.

Priam's sons. Thersites accused Achilles of violating the body, and himself put out its eyes with his spear. For this, or possibly for stealing some treasure, Achilles killed him, knocking off his head with one blow. Though Thersites in the *Iliad* is a deformed demagogue properly chastised by Odysseus, he was in fact a kinsman of Diomede, and his death caused dissension in the Greek camp.

Achilles was shot in his vulnerable heel by Paris in a battle at the gates of Troy. Apollo guided the shaft, for in a shame culture success as well as failure is projected on to the gods to avoid personal responsibility disruptive of society, just as ritual killings are always 'accidental'. A later romantic version told of Achilles' love for Priam's daughter, Polyxena, and of secret and treacherous meetings and betrayals. This atmosphere of dissension and failure can even be detected in the *Iliad*, where the Greeks on occasions contemplate withdrawal. Clearly the expedition was not an unqualified success.

Achilles' arms were awarded to Odysseus, and not to Ajax who, at the loss of more face than he could reasonably be expected to bear, turned on himself the aggression which social pressures prevented him from directing against the Greek leaders, and committed suicide. He found some difficulty as Heracles is said to have made him invulnerable in all but one part of his body by wrapping him in the lion's skin. The body of Ajax was buried, not burnt, and he was the object of cult both in the Troad, where his grave was by the sea side and contained huge bones, and at Salamis his home, where it was associated with that of his son Eurysaces, 'Broad Shield'. There was a story that the armour of Achilles was washed ashore from the shipwreck of Odysseus, and came to rest on Ajax's grave in the Troad.

The Greeks then brought to Troy the helper necessary to the successful conclusion of the enterprise, Philoctetes with the bow of Heracles. The Trojan Helenus, who had quarrelled

with his brother for the hand of Helen after Paris' death, revealed three further conditions: that the bones of Pelops should be returned to Asia Minor whence he came, that the son of Achilles should fight, and that the Palladium, a magic image of Athena, should be stolen. Neoptolemus was fetched from Scyros, where he had been begotten, and, clad in his father's armour, was prominent in the sack of Troy: the motif suggests the success of the sons of the Seven against Thebes.

The Palladium was said to have been made by Athena to represent her female companion Pallas, whom she accidentally killed and whose name she took. Zeus cast it down to Troy where Ilus built it a temple. It had to be stolen because no city can be taken as long as its gods remain in it. The Romans, who claimed that Aeneas had brought the real Palladium to Rome, had a special ceremony of evocation to entice enemy gods to Rome. So Odysseus and Diomede stole it as they had joined in killing the horses of Rhesus. Odysseus used the trick of disguising himself as a beggar and enlisting the help of Helen.

He also devised the wooden horse in which the heroes entered Troy by a trick. It may be a recollection of some kind of siege engine, which breached the walls at, no doubt, the one place where they had not been built by gods and were therefore vulnerable – another device for throwing the responsibility of defeat off the defenders. Or it may represent treachery in Troy, the normal way in which the Greeks took walled cities: certainly Antenor and Aeneas were spared by the Greeks, though they were needed for genealogical reasons. All the Greeks but those in the horse retired to Tenedos, pretending that they were finally withdrawing and that the horse was a thanks-offering to Athena (though it ought to have been to Poseidon, who built the walls and often appears in the form of a horse). The Trojans dragged it into the city, of course disbelieving the prophecies of Cassandra and also neglecting the ambiguous warning of Apollo, who sent two snakes to devour the sons of Laocoon, who had begotten them on his wife in the sanctuary.

The Greeks in the horse, whose number varies from twenty-three to

three thousand, were all frightened except for Neoptolemus. Their presence was suspected by Helen, who went round addressing each in the tones of his wife. Odysseus bade them all keep silence and strangled Anticlus, the only one who was going to cry out. Helen was accompanied by her second husband, Deiphobus, and her role is ambiguous, for 'some god wanted to give glory to the Trojans'.

The first out of the horse was killed leaping down. The rest admitted the Greek army, which had been guided from Tenedos by a beacon lighted on the grave of Achilles. The Greeks sacked the sleeping city, not without impieties. Neoptolemus slew Priam at the altar of Zeus where he had taken refuge. Locrian Ajax raped Cassandra before the image of Athena. As-

tyanax, infant son of Hector, was cast from the battlements like a sacrifice. And Polyxena was sacrificed on the tomb of Achilles, the germ of the romantic story of their love.

Amazonomachies, the fight between Greeks and the female warriors, the Amazons, either at Troy, where they sent a contingent to help Priam, or when they invaded Athens, became a favourite sculptural motif in the fourth century, replacing the battle of Lapiths and Centaurs as a symbol of the triumph of Hellenism over barbarism (as seen in the metopes from the Parthenon in the British Museum). The change, however, was more for artistic reasons than mythological. Where the fifth century was interested in horses, the fourth added women, and the Amazonomachy provided opportunities for both, since Amazons were often mounted, and the woman can be depicted in a more active role than, as on the pediment at Olympia, in the passive one of Lapith women carried off by centaurs. So a warrior fighting an Amazon was an appropriate decoration for a ceremonial breastplate. Here the eye contact between the warrior and the presumably dying Amazon suggests an identification as Achilles and Penthesilea. British Museum, London.

The End of the Heroes

Perhaps because of their various acts of impiety, few of the heroes had a safe or profitable return home, with the exception of Diomede and Nestor. Menelaus was at first determined to kill Helen for her infidelity, but because of her beauty (and her divine status) was unable to do so, and set out with the other two. But he was delayed by the death of his helmsman off Sunium, and off the south-west promontory of the Peloponnese a north-westerly drove him to Crete and Egypt. He spent the next eight years accumulating wealth in the eastern Méditerranean. Finally he was becalmed off Pharos, an uninhabited off-shore island which the *Odyssey* envisages as a long sail from Egypt, to which Menelaus had to return, on the advice of Proteus, an Old Man of the Sea, before he could make Sparta. All early navigation depended on starting from a known landmark. At home he continued to live in immense prosperity with his divine wife, looking forward to the Islands of the Blest. Most of this is a realistic account of freebooting true enough of any period from the Mycenaean to the eighth century.

Some of the Greeks did not return at all. Calchas the prophet went to Colophon overland, to die in a kind of magical conflict (a folk-tale motif) with Mopsus, the son of a 'bride of Apollo', Manto the daughter of Tiresias. She had emigrated there with some Argives after the capture of Thebes by the sons of the Seven (one of the central episodes in the Theban Cycle of myths). The contest was to guess the number of figs on a tree, and the number of pigs in a sow's unborn farrow. The story is Ionian propaganda in favour of the local oracle of Apollo near Colophon.

The impious Ajax, like Menelaus, suffered shipwreck. Ancient scholars tried to fix the exact time and date of the fall of Troy. It may have taken place dangerously late in the summer, at the setting of the Pleiads, when the sailing season ends in Greece and the autumn winds begin to blow. Thus there may be a perfectly natural explanation of these calamities. Ajax succeeded in getting to shore and boasted that he had escaped against the will of the immortal gods, who promptly proved him wrong. Poseidon broke off the rock upon which he was sitting and drowned him. An annual Locrian ceremony, in which a fire ship was launched with black sails, was explained as mourning for the dead Ajax.

A number of the Greeks returned to find that they had been supplanted in the affections of their wives during their absence. This happened to Idomeneus of Crete, but another or additional story was told to account for his exile, that to escape from a storm he vowed to sacrifice the first thing he met on his return, which was of course his son or daughter. A plague resulting from this impious sacrifice led the people to banish him. In this folk-tale motif of the Homecomer's Vow, the order of events had been deliberately altered to conceal the normality of the practice, and to absolve Idomeneus of the responsibility for having willed it.

The Death of Agamemnon

The classic case of the betrayed husband is Agamemnon himself, who was supplanted by Aegisthus, who had already killed Atreus, his father's brother. In seducing his cousin's wife, Aegisthus was only doing what Thyestes had done to Atreus. He may

Left. Purification of Orestes. This fourth century south Italian vase shows the two chief figures, Orestes and Apollo. Orestes, with his conical hat off his head, clasps the navel stone with the left arm, in which he holds his scabbard, and with the sword in his right wards off an invisible Fury. Apollo performs the purification with two laurel leaves which he has dipped in the bowl full of presumably pig's blood. British Museum, London.

Opposite. Murder of Aegisthus. This painting of the murder is earlier (500–475 B.C.) than any of the surviving dramatic treatments of the story. It suggests that Orestes came openly and armed, though Aegisthus, who is dragged off his throne, was evidently not expecting the attack. The horrified girl is Chrysothemis, the younger sister who stayed with her mother, and not Electra, who is associated with the murder only in drama. Kunsthistorisches Museum, Vienna.

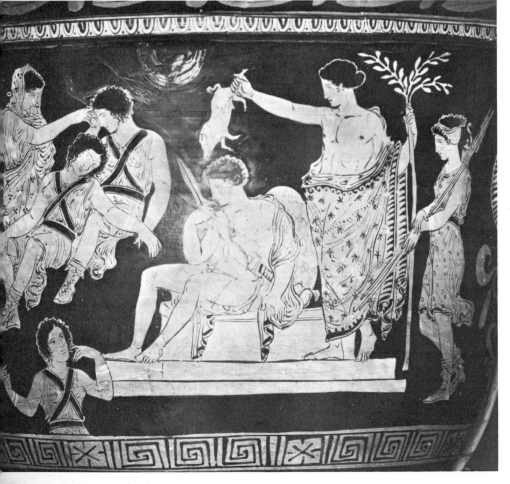

Left. Orestes and the Furies. This early Apulian bell crater from the beginning of the fourth century B.C. is one of the most dramatic illustrations of the story of Orestes, a favourite subject. The painting seems to be closely related to Aeschylus' play the *Eumenides*. The ghost of Clytemnestra is seen awaking the sleeping Furies, showing that the purification performed by Apollo is powerless against the ancient curse of blood. Apollo, half girt in a richly embroidered tragic garment, holds his bay in one hand and in the other a pig over the head of Orestes, not to illustrate but to symbolise the purification he has performed with its blood; for the purification was not shown on stage. Musée du Louvre, Paris.

have had some real claim to the kingdom. The murder of Agamemnon is simply an episode in the gory history of the Pelopids. It contains elements derived ultimately from ritual: for Clytemnestra murdered him in the bath-house after a bath, striking him three blows, possibly with a double axe, after catching him in a hunting net more appropriate to a sacred animal than to a man.

Zeus, through the oracle of his son Apollo at Delphi, ordered Orestes to

avenge the murder of his father by killing his mother Clytemnestra and her lover Aegisthus. He did so and returned from exile with the help of his almost incestuously devoted sister Electra and under the protection of Hermes. Orestes was purified of the murder of his mother by Apollo at Delphi. But the Furies were unaffected and continued to pursue him. Orestes fled to Athens and took refuge at the image of Athena, who instituted the Athenian homicide court of the Areopagus to decide the issue. Her own presiding vote went to Orestes. This made the votes equal, and, according to the practice of the court, Orestes was aquitted. The Furies were persuaded to accept cult at Athens, becoming the Kindly Ones, Eumenides, earth-goddesses rather like the daughters of Cecrops.

Iphigenia had been carried off to the Crimea. Orestes went there to bring back his sister to Athens with the image of Artemis. He was taken prisoner and Iphigenia recognised her brother only in the nick of time to prevent his sacrifice.

Odysseus

The fate of Agamemnon, and the filial duty of Orestes, are in the *Odyssey* contrasted with that of Odysseus, and held up as a model to his son Telemachus. Odysseus returned from Troy after ten years of wanderings, to find his substance being devoured by the nobility of Ithaca, who were

pressing his wife Penelope to marry one of them. She kept them at bay until his return by insisting that she must finish the shroud she was weaving for Odysseus' father Laertes. This shroud she unpicked each night. Odysseus returned in time to defeat all the suitors in the exploit to determine Penelope's husband. He used a great bow, which he alone was able to string, to shoot them down at a feast.

The story of the Return of Odysseus is made up of a number of different traditional versions of what may have been originally the myth of the supplanter. In some of them Penelope seems to have recognised her husband by some token and to have connived in the destruction of his rivals. But the poet has transferred this to the aged nurse, who recognises Odysseus by a scar on his thigh, and to the faithful hound Argus, who dies after greeting his master. Even after the suitors have been slain, Penelope refuses to believe it is her husband returned until she has tested him by claiming that his marriage bed has been moved, an impossibility since

Odysseus in making it had incorporated an olive tree which grew on the site of his palace.

The myths in the *Odyssey* appear in the account of his wanderings which Odysseus gives at the court of the Phaeacians, a race of idealised sailors whose swift and silent ships find their own way and may once have ferried men to the land of the dead. Angered at their habit of giving free passage to all, including his enemy Odysseus, Poseidon turned their ship into a rock on its return, a myth that explains natural features of an island traditionally identified as Corfu. Odysseus was cast up there by a shipwreck and befriended by the king's daughter Nausicaa. He defeated all the Phaeacian nobles in an athletic contest. The episode is clearly modelled on the myth of the supplanter. Only the exigencies of the plot prevent him from marrying Nausicaa.

He does appear however as the temporary consort of two nymphs or goddesses in the course of his wanderings. Many of the motifs that occur during his journey seem to have been taken from the Argonautic saga, and may contain some information about northern waters. But they all seem to be located in the western Mediterranean, an area in which the Greeks showed increasing interest from the eighth century. It was also the scene of some of the exploits of Heracles.

After leaving Troy, Odysseus touched at Thrace, where he sacked the city of the Cicones, sparing only the priest of Apollo, who gave him in return some exceptional wine that could be diluted with twenty parts of water. Thence he was blown to North Africa, to the land of the Lotus-eaters, whose food caused all that tasted it to forget home and family. Then in Sicily the Cyclops Polyphemus imprisoned him in his cave and ate his companions. Odysseus made him drunk with his Thracian wine and put out his one eye, escaping in the morning under the belly of the Cyclops' ram.

The Cyclops were originally the smiths of Zeus, who made the thunderbolt. For the purposes of the

Odyssey they have been turned into uncivilised shepherds, sons of Poseidon, whose anger Odysseus provokes by blinding Polyphemus. But they have retained the single eye typical of smiths which is necessary to the plot. The traditional motif of the magic ring, which betrays the position of the escaped hero to the blinded giant and can be removed only with the finger on which it has been put, is absent. Instead Odysseus betrays himself and his name by his own boasting. He had previously concealed it and tricked the Cyclops by saying that he was 'No man'. But he succeeded in escaping the rocks which the Cyclops hurled at him and proceeded to the next adventure.

Aeolus, king of the winds, got him within sight of Ithaca by tying up all the contrary winds in a goatskin. Then Odysseus went to sleep, and his comrades, thinking the sack contained treasure, untied it so that they were blown back west again. They reached the land of the giant cannibal Laestrygonians. Some of Odysseus' comrades encounter the king's daughter, but little is made of the episode because Odysseus must be preserved for further adventures, in the extreme west.

There lay the island of Circe, daughter of the Sun. Circe turned Odysseus' comrades into pigs, but Odysseus was protected against her spells by the magic herb moly which Hermes found for him. It must originally have been the Herb of Life, and Circe the enchanter's daughter who assists the hero in his quest. But all the ritual elements which lie behind these stories have been converted into fiction. Odysseus did, however, become the consort of Circe, after threatening her with his sword and making her swear not to harm him. She sent him to consult the soul of Tiresias so that Odysseus as a typical hero descended into Hades, where he encountered his own crew-man Elpenor who had taken a swift route to Hades by falling to his death off the roof of Circe's palace.

On his way back from Aeaea, Circe's island, Odysseus safely passed by the Sirens, stopping the ears of the rowers with wax and having himself tied to the mast. He also survived the monsters Scylla and Charybdis, whom he preferred to the Clashing Rocks which only the Argo could survive. Scylla was a kind of monstrous bitch rather like a giant squid, with twelve feet and six long necks, each with a horrible head on it with three rows of teeth. Even so she was better than Charybdis, the whirlpool which sucked in water and belched it out again three times a day. Scylla and Charybdis are traditionally located in the straits of Messina between Italy and Sicily, but they may equally well be tales deliberately told by Phoenician sailors to keep the Greeks from passing the Strait of Gibraltar. Odysseus steered close to Scylla, accepting the loss of six of his men to save the ship and the rest.

But Odysseus' companions finally met their fate through their own folly when they killed and ate the magic cattle of the Sun, a type of impiety more usually committed by Giants. Zeus struck the ship with a thunderbolt, but allowed Odysseus, who is necessary to the plot, to survive clinging to the mast. It was sucked into Charybdis and belched out again, while Odysseus clung to a wild fig tree which grew above the whirlpool. From there he was cast up on the island of Calypso, the Hider, who kept him as her unwilling consort for seven years until the gods told her to send him home on a raft. Poseidon wrecked the raft, but Odysseus was saved by the White Goddess Leucothea. She gave him her veil which carried him safely to the land of the Phaeacians. Landing there with the help of a kindly river god, he threw the veil back into the sea, doubtless without looking back, and the goddess took it up again.

Thus Odysseus survived all his

Left. Odysseus in Circe's house. The vigorous free style employed on vases from 450 B.C., even when very sketchy in style, as here, could produce an effective illustration of action. Odysseus rises from his chair and draws his sword when Circe tries to turn him into a beast, like his companions behind him, one with a pig's head, one with an ass's. The herb moly, given him by Hermes, had rendered Odysseus immune to her spells, and she flees before him, dropping the mixing bowl in which she had mixed the wine, and the rod with which she had stirred it. Metropolitan Museum of Art, New York. Gift of Amelia E. White, 1941.

wanderings and came back safely to Ithaca to reclaim his kingdom. Then he set out on his travels again, to keep his vows. Following Tiresias' instructions, he found the people who took an oar for a winnowing fan in north-west Greece. There he married the queen of the Thesprotians, only returning to Ithaca when his son by her was old enough to inherit the kingdom. The later Thesprotians claimed their descent from Odysseus, and told this story to account for it.

In Ithaca finally he met his death at the hand of his son by Circe, Telegonus. He came to Ithaca to seek his father and 'accidentally' slew him with a spear tipped with the spine of a sting-ray, the gentle death from the sea which Tiresias had prophesied for him. When Telegonus discovered what he had done he took the corpse to Circe, who made it immortal. He married Penelope and Telemachus married Circe. Circe's other son by Odysseus was said to be Latinus, by whose daughter Aeneas became ancestor of the Romans.

Neoptolemus

Most of these stories are typical of the later continuations of the great epics. Many of them are fictions to provide a respectable heroic ancestry for later peoples, though they may contain some genuine ritual survivals. It is, however, significant that Odysseus had no successor in Ithaca. Almost all the heroic dynasties died out in the generation after the Trojan War. Neoptolemus joined up with Helenus, the renegade Trojan soothsayer who had told the Greeks the conditions that they had to fulfil before Troy could be taken, and had caused them to send for Neoptolemus. Either on his advice or that of Thetis, he avoided shipwreck by returning to Greece by land through Epirus. There he became king over the Molossians, having been advised to settle where he found a house with foundations of iron, walls of wood and a roof of wool.

Neoptolemus found the Molossians camping under blankets or fleeces supported on spears of which the iron tips were stuck into the ground. There he begot them an ancestor Molossus on Andromache, who had been his share of the Trojan spoils. He returned to Phthia and reclaimed his kingdom from the sons of Acastus, who had expelled Peleus. But even though in one version he married Hermione, daughter of Helen and Menelaus, Neoptolemus got no son to succeed him there, and died in sordid circumstances at Delphi, brawling with the attendants over the flesh of the offerings. The story may conceal the last ritual death of a hero in Greek mythology: for Neoptolemus was killed with a sacrificial knife and buried near the temple of Apollo, who was responsible for his death. There he received annual offerings as a hero.

The Return of the Heraclids

Orestes is the only one of these heroes who was succeeded by a son. This was Tisamenus, and when he was king of Sparta the Heraclids (descendants of Heracles) returned to the

The Mycenaeans had over-extended themselves in the unsettled period at the end of the second millennium. Their settlements over the eastern Mediterranean may have weakened them at home, and their strength seems to have been further dissipated by freebooting and viking ventures. Such ventures are represented in myth by the siege of Troy and in history by the concerted attack on Egypt by the 'Peoples of the Sea', which was repulsed by Rameses II in 1192 B.C. though it is not certain that any Greeks took part in it.

If the later presence of a different form of Greek in much of the Peloponnese and in Boeotia is the result of the migration of new tribes the weakness of the Mycenaean dynasties may have given the opportunity to such bands of Greeks to make their way by land and sea into the rich pasture lands of Boeotia and the Peloponnese, driving out the existing inhabitants to settle in Asia Minor, or confining them to the poorer lands of Attica and Arcadia. They replaced the great Mycenaean palaces with more primitive settlements where small closely-knit patriarchal families combined. The sack which preserved in its flames the current accounts of the Mycenaean kingdom of Nestor at Pylos, written on clay, may represent an episode in the invasion of the Dorians, as the newcomers are called from their dialect. But traces and traditions of the earlier period survived in the stories which the Greeks continued to tell, and which they brought to an end with their own version of the Dorian Invasion, the Return of the Heraclids.

Peloponnese for their inheritance. At Heracles' death they had fled from Eurystheus and found only the Athenians to protect them. Eurystheus was slain in a battle in Attica and his head and his body were buried separately, like those of the husbands of the Danaids, to protect the strategic routes to Athens. Then the Heraclids returned, but were driven out by a plague and told by an oracle to await the third crop before trying again. They took this to mean the third year, and were again repulsed when Hyllus, a son of Heracles, was defeated in single combat at the Isthmus.

A hundred years later the Heraclids received the same oracle, now interpreted to mean the third generation, and they were advised to cross the Corinthian Gulf and take the Three-Eyed Man as guide. After some trouble caused by the murder of a soothsayer, they crossed from Naupactus, which took its name from the ships they built there, in three tribes led by four descendants of Heracles, Temenus, Cresphontes and the twin sons of Aristomachus. They found a man sitting on a one-eyed horse. With him as their guide, they defeated Tisamenus and killed him.

They took possession of the whole of the Peloponnese, for which they drew lots, setting up three altars to the Zeus of their fathers, first for Argos, then for Sparta and lastly for Messene. Cresphontes wanted Messene, and so he cast into the pitcher of water not a stone but a piece of mud. The mud dissolved, so that the lots of the other two were bound to come out first, and he got what he wanted. Temenus got Argos, and the twin sons Sparta, where the dual kingship survived. On the altars they found signs which foretold the subsequent history of the three regions, a toad for Argos, to warn them to stay at home, a wily fox for Messene, but a serpent for the Spartans who were terrible in attack.

Postscript

Since this book was first issued in 1969 there have been a number of new interpretations of myth, and some of the approaches made then have been called in question. The 'explanations' of Greek mythology advanced at the time were psychological and anthropological – the former unrepentantly Freudian, the latter perhaps excessively Frazerian though making use also of some later ideas.

The work of Robert Graves was also acknowledged. He is the author of what is still the most popular account of Greek myth but the one most often attacked by professional scholars. This is because of its systematic interpretation of the evidence supporting the view that all Greek myths give an historical account of an early matrilinear and feminist society, and of its modification by an intrusive patriarchal male dominated society worshipping a father-god.

Greek myths were told in Archaic and Classical Greece in the only form we now have them and the belief that they may contain evidence for an earlier quite different social structure is a variety of the doctrine of 'survivals' formulated by early scholars of folk-lore. This argues that 'survivals' of earlier social structures might be preserved in myths – in story patterns felt to be appropriate. An example (mentioned in the Introduction) from fairy tales is the story of the youngest son who has to successfully perform the tasks (perhaps a 'survival' of the system of ultimogeniture, by which the youngest son inherits as likely to be the most vigorous in a period of short life expectancy) and wins the princess with half the kingdom (perhaps a 'survival' of matrilinear succession) with whom he lives 'happily ever after' (not a survival but a piece of wishful thinking).

It is also possible to interpret many of these elements which have been seen as evidence for an earlier social structure as really reflecting 'hard cases' in the culture in which the myths were told. Thus, in a patrilinear society, the heiress is an anomalous case. Her marriage in the normal way to a man from another family extinguishes the male line of her father. It was to avoid this that the law, in fifth-century Athens, insisted that an heiress be married, after her father's death, to a male relative in the male line. Another solution, applied during the father's life, is for him to adopt his son-in-law, thus ensuring the survival of the name. At a psychological level, the marriage of a daughter may be felt by the father as a betrayal of himself: he would prefer his 'favourite daughter', who was, as a child, encouraged to express her love for him by wanting to 'marry Daddy when I grow up' and so gratify his suppressed incestuous desires, to remain unmarried and look after him instead of abandoning him for a younger man and committing with him the ultimate parricide – 'I'll be alive when you're dead'.

These two fears, the extinction of the line by the marriage of an heiress and the betrayal of the father by a daughter's marriage are exactly those which appear transmogrified in the common mythological situation in which the king fears death at the hands of his daughter's husband or of her son, a fate which he cannot avoid, however he tries. Either a god begets a son on an imprisoned daughter (as Zeus on Danae) or a suitor eventually fulfils the impossible tasks and actually kills the king (as Pelops did to Oenomaus): and the exposed child, like Perseus, always survives, eventually to kill his grandfather. The myth enables the hearer to acknowledge his fears by confronting them in a mythological situation, and thus to find and accept a legal and psychological solution.

The 'hard cases' may not be confined to the culture which originated the myth. The position of women is a live issue in our culture today, and this accounts for the willingness of students of Greek mythology to find in it evidence for an earlier and ideal state of matrilinear succession or even of matriarchy. Matrilinear succession is indeed an attested way of organising males, who always retain the executive powers. Matriarchy is a different matter: it is a reverse guilt fantasy generated in male minds by the treatment of women as disposable chattels. There are no such fantasies of matriarchy in Greek mythology, only that of an entirely female society of Amazons. There are, however, especially in Greek tragedy, a number of 'terrible women' who usurp male roles and are not content with docile acceptance of their lot: such are Clytemnestra, Medea and even Antigone, who murder husband or children and defy the rules of the state.

Two other areas are currently highly sensitive in our culture, those of human sacrifice and cannibalism. The latter is now seen as an imperialist myth imposed on non-white cultures to justify their exploitation (W. Arens, *The Man-Eating Myth*, New York 1979). In Greek mythology it is usually linked with the killing of children, as of Pelops, offered to the gods as food by his father Tantalus, or the sons of Thyestes offered to their father by Atreus as a deliberate act of revenge. Human sacrifice, in Greek myth, is normally that of a daughter, like Iphigenia, but there is a good deal of evidence both in mythology and in ritual which has suggested that human sacrifice was once practised in Greece.

But once again the mythological, and even the ritual evidence is ambiguous. In an area so charged with emotion we may be dealing not with evidence of 'survival' for fact, but with fantasy. So great is the emotion generated by these topics even today that when a Greek and an English archaeologist found what they have interpreted as evidence for actual human sacrifice and cannibalism at Arkhanes near Knossos and at Knossos itself, they provoked a strong adverse public reaction for attributing to the idealised and peace-loving

Minoans such a barbaric, disgusting custom. Scholars too are unwilling to accept the evidence as unequivocal: sacrifice will be hard to establish without a good forensic pathologist, preferably dealing with a bound victim with the knife still between his ribs, as perhaps at Arkhanes.

These examples, from different and sensitive areas, indicate some of the pitfalls in the way of applying the doctrine of 'survivals' to Greek mythology. There are similar pitfalls in the way of the use of anthropological evidence. Classical scholars (and perhaps others) tend to employ the concepts of other disciplines some time later than they are first propounded, and often after they have been abandoned and superseded in their parent disciplines. In this book, the terms 'shame culture' and 'guilt culture' are employed to contrast two ethical systems, which are related to two different forms of family organisation outlined in the Introduction. These terms were taken from the study by E. R. Dodds, *The Greeks and the irrational*, noted in the 'Further Reading List', who had himself taken them from American anthropologists of the inter-war period, notably Ruth Benedict. But modern anthropologists no longer employ them, and question their validity. Nonetheless, applied with caution they may illuminate episodes which are otherwise obscure.

More recent scholars have followed the French anthropologist Claude Lévi-Strauss in applying to Greek mythology the concepts and techniques of the doctrine known as Structuralism. The best simple account of the method is given by Edmund Leach in his volume on Lévi-Strauss in the Modern Masters series of Fontana (1970). For Lévi-Strauss it is the structure of the myth that is important, and this can be appreciated in any of its re-tellings, even modern ones in translation or in a foreign language: myths are used to cope with contradictions in thought and in society generated by the natu-

ral tendency of the human mind to think in terms of opposites (as a computer works by a binary system of switching – on/off or yes/no). In the myth of Oedipus he has noted that all three generations bear names which indicate some form of deformity, Labdacus lame – or perhaps better stuttering –, Laius left-sided or left-handed, and Oedipus 'Swellfoot' (a condition explained in the myth by his exposure with his ankles pierced). The contradiction which he finds especially in the myth of Oedipus himself is that between the 'over-' or 'under-valuation' of kinship – incest and parricide! G. S. Kirk practises a modified and empirical structuralist approach to some myths in his books *Myth, its meaning and functions in ancient and other cultures* (Cambridge 1970) and *The Nature of Greek myths* (Pelican 1974).

But Lévi-Strauss's structuralist approach has itself already been superseded in its country of origin, at least as a tool for literary criticism, by movements calling themselves Post-Structuralist, notably the Deconstructionist approach of Derrida, for whom the text is not a means of communication between the author and the reader but an independent object into which the reader may put what meaning he chooses.

Most recently of all, W. Burkert, whose analysis of the myth of the Argonauts and the Lemnian women is cited with approval in the present work, has turned to the fashionable new discipline of human ethology (*The Naked Ape* and *Man-watching*) to trace some myths and religious rituals back to behaviour patterns attributable to the hunting bands of Palaeolithic man, in *Structure and history in Greek mythology and ritual* (University of California Press 1979).

The concern for explanations, and the desire to make them in the terms of current intellectual conceptions illustrates the continuing vitality of Greek myth. Lévi-Strauss more than anybody has recognised that it is the

story-pattern which makes for this vitality, even though he himself totally rejects a diachronic approach: – a historical approach using story patterns and their modifications to provide evidence of practices and beliefs (not necessarily consciously present to the mind of the teller) for the period of that re-telling and even for earlier periods. But the difficulties, as indicated above, in using the evidence of myth in this way prove that any evidence can only be used inside an agreed frame of intellectual reference. If, for example, human sacrifice, cannibalism or matrilinear structures are deemed impossible within that frame, then even the strongest apparent evidence for them in myth must be otherwise interpreted.

Myth, like other forms of imaginative literature, is always significant and important for the culture that makes use of it, and is always related to the system of values of that culture, and, whatever its apparent subject, expresses and recommends a view of the world. Myth differs from other forms of imaginative literature in that this expression is made not through the literary form of a particular re-telling alone but also through the raw structure and subject matter of the myth. That is why the myth even of cultures as alien from us as the Japanese or that of the Brazilian Indians studied by Lévi-Strauss can still have some meaning for the Western world. But Greek mythology has, historically, been part of the culture of that world ever since its first literary emergence in Homer and the Attic tragedians, transmitted to us first through the Latin literature of the Romans who took it over, then through translations of that Latin literature, and recently through translations and re-tellings (like this book and others in the Further Reading List) direct from the original Greek. That continues to guarantee its primacy among the myths of the world for us, the members of that culture.

Further Reading List

Dictionaries and works of reference:
Smith, W. (ed.) *A Dictionary of Greek and Roman Biography and Mythology*. 3 vol., London 1876: still the most exhaustive work in English.
Cary, M., etc. (ed.) *The Oxford Classical Dictionary*. Oxford 1949.
Rose, H. J. *A Handbook of Greek Mythology*. Methuen, 1958 and also in Methuen's University Paperbacks.

Greek myths have been retold at various levels and for different classes of readers many times since the Renaissance. Recent examples are:
Graves, R. *Greek Myths*. Cassell and Penguin, many reprints since the first editions of 1958 and 1955 respectively.
Grant, M. *Myths of the Greeks and Romans*. Weidenfeld and Nicolson, 1962; Mentor Books, New English Library, 1965.
Simpson, M. *Gods and Heroes of the Greeks*. University of Massachusetts, 1976.
Michael ffolkes *ffolkes' Cartoon Companion to Classical Mythology*. David & Charles, 1978.

General books on mythology and Greek culture:
Frazer, Sir J. G. *The Golden Bough*, abridged edition. Macmillan, 1922 and subsequent reprints.
Harrison, Jane. *Prolegomena to the Study of Greek Religion*. Cambridge University Press, 1903; 3rd edition 1932; Merlin Press 1961.

Harrison, Jane. *Themis: A Study of the Social Origins of Greek Religion*. Cambridge University Press, 1912; 2nd edition 1927; Merlin Press, 1963.
Murray, Gilbert. 'Early Greek Epic', in *Anthropology and the Classics*, ed. Marett, R. R. Oxford University Press, 1908.
Harrison, Jane. *Mythology*. Harrap.
Halliday, W. R. *Greek and Roman Folklore*. Harrap, 1927.
Rose, H. J. *Primitive Culture in Greece*. Methuen, 1925.
Halliday, W. R. *Indo-European Folk-Tales and Greek Legend*. Cambridge University Press, 1933.
Senior, M. *Greece and its Myths*. Gollancz, 1978.
Meyer, Reinhold. *Past and Present: The Continuity of Classical Myths*. Hakkert, Toronto, 1972.
Slater, Philip E. *The Glory of Hera: Greek Mythology and the Greek Family*. Beacon Press, Boston, 1968.
Page, Denys. *Folktales in Homer's Odyssey*. Harvard University Press, 1978.
Fotenrose, Joseph. *Python, a study of Delphic man and its origin*. California University Press, 1959.
Campbell, Joseph. *The Hero with a thousand faces*. Abacus, 1975.
Dodds, E. R. *The Greeks and the Irrational*. University of California Press, 1951; 2nd edition 1959 also in paperback.
Lindsay, Jack. *The clashing rocks*. Chapman & Hall, 1965.

Butterworth, E. A. S. *Some Traces of the pre-Olympian World in Greek Literature and Myth*. de Gruyter, Berlin 1966.
Röhde, E. *Psyche*. Routledge and Kegan Paul, 8th edition, 1925; reprinted 1950.

Psychological studies
Kerenyi, C. *The Gods of the Greeks*. Thames & Hudson, 1951 and *The Heroes of the Greeks*. Thames & Hudson, 1959.
Otto, W. F. *The Homeric Gods*. Thames & Hudson, 1955.
Stokes, Adrian. *Greek Culture and the Ego*. Tavistock Publications Ltd, 1958.

Studies of particular myths:
Harrison, Jane. *Myths of the Odyssey in Art and Literature*. London, 1882; with M. de G. Verrall. *Mythology and Monuments of ancient Athens*. Macmillan, 1890.
Hartland, E. S. *The Legend of Perseus*. London, 1894-1896.
Bacon, J. R. *The Voyage of the Argonauts*. Methuen, 1925.
Lindsay, Jack. *Helen of Troy*. Constable, 1974.
Nilsson, M. P. *Mycenean Origin of Greek Mythology*. Cambridge University Press, 1932; Oldbourne, 1964.
Brown, N. O. *Hermes the Thief, (the Evolution of a Myth)*. University of Wisconsin Press, 1947.
Woodward, J. M. *Perseus: a Study in Greek Art and Legend*. Cambridge University Press, 1937.

Acknowledgments

Photographs. Archives Photographiques, Paris 33 left; Ashmolean Museum, Oxford 12 left, 28 bottom, 40, 88 right, 110 left; Bavaria Verlag – Konrad Helbig 31; Bavaria Verlag – W. K. Müller 11, 58; Bavaria Verlag – M. Pedone 14-15; Bavaria Verlag – Dietrich Hans Teuffen 69; Bibliothèque Nationale, Paris 124 top; Boissonnas, Geneva 7 left, 38; British Museum, London 29 bottom, 52, 62, 63 bottom, 71, 79 bottom, 81 bottom, 88 left, 89 bottom left, 93 top, 102, 108 centre, 109, 112, 118, 123 bottom, 129, 132 top, 137; F. Bruckmann Verlag, Munich 20 top; J. Allan Cash, London 82-83, 104 top; Deutsches Archäologisches Institut, Athens 20 bottom, 66; Photographie Giraudon, Paris 39, 86, 94-95; Hamlyn Group Picture Library 6, 50, 83 left, 83 right, 107, 111; Hermitage Museum, Leningrad 64 top; Hirmer Fotoarchiv, Munich 1, 12 centre, 12 right, 21, 22 top, 22 bottom, 25, 28 top left, 28 top right, 32 right, 34 top, 34 bottom left, 34 bottom right, 47, 49 bottom, 54, 55, 63 top left, 63 top right, 64 bottom, 65, 70, 73, 74, 85 top, 85 bottom, 90 top, 92-93, 93 bottom, 101 top, 103, 104 bottom, 108 top, 114, 115 top, 115 bottom, 116 left, 116 right, 117 left, 120, 127 top, 128, 138; Michael Holford, Loughton 23, 26, 30, 79 top, 87, 90 bottom, 98, 130; Kunsthistorisches Museum, Vienna 133; Larousse, Paris 91; Mansell Collection, London 7 right; Mansell – Alinari 48, 132 bottom; Mansell – Anderson 81 top, 96 top left; Mansell – Giraudon 29 top, 80; Metropolitan Museum of Art, New York 13 top, 13 bottom, 44, 53 top, 57, 75, 77, 117 right, 122, 125, 136 bottom; Museum für Kunst und Geschichte, Hamburg 45; Museum of Fine Arts, Boston, Massachusetts 22 centre, 24 top right, 32 left, 49 top, 53 bottom, 89 top, 95, 96 top right, 96 bottom, 127 centre, 127 bottom, 134; National Museum, Copenhagen 123 top, 124 bottom; Picturepoint, London 8, 18, 27, 33 right, 101 bottom; Scala, Antella 2, 19, 35, 43, 51, 59, 67, 78-79, 99, 119, 135; Staatliche Antikensammlungen und Glyptothek, Munich 17, 60, 89 bottom right, 108 bottom, 110 right; Soprintendza alle Antichità della Calabria, Reggio di Calabria 24 top left; Soprintendenza alle Antichità delle Sicilia Orientale, Syracuse 24 bottom; Soprintendenza alle Antichità dell'Etruria, Florence 84, 126; Staatliche Museen Antikenabteilung, Berlin 16, 97; Nick Stournaras, Athens 136 top; Roger-Viollet, Paris 100, 105.

The illustration on page 121 is from John Boardman *Engraved Gems: The Ionides Collection*, Thames and Hudson, 1968, photograph by Robert L. Wilkins.

Index

References in *italic type* indicate a caption entry.